Hospital Information System (HIS) Project Success

Hospital Information System (HIS) Project Success addresses one of the most persistent challenges in healthcare centers: why Hospital Information System (HIS) projects continue to struggle despite massive investments, growing regulatory demands, and rapid digital transformation.

Drawing on nearly two decades of hands-on HIS implementation and operational experience, the author offers a clear, actionable framework for hospital managers, CIOs, IT managers, and project teams to achieve HIS project success. The core of the book is the Core Interaction Model (CIM), a performance-driven cycle that integrates observation, implementation, and qualification to support both project delivery and long-term system excellence. By adapting well-known project management methodologies and Agile to the unique realities of healthcare environments, CIM bridges the gap between strategy, governance, and daily operations. What makes this book beneficial is its practical, experience-based approach that connects digital health strategy with real-world HIS project challenges.

The book synthesizes best practices with lived experience, offering tools, examples, and insights that reflect the complexities of actual hospital environments rather than idealized scenarios.

Hospital Information System (HIS) Project Success

A Practical Guide in the Digital Era

Shahram Gharib

Routledge
Taylor & Francis Group
A PRODUCTIVITY PRESS BOOK

Designed cover image: Elise Harpin

First published 2027
by Routledge
605 Third Avenue, New York, NY 10158

and by Routledge
4 Park Square, Milton Park, Abingdon, Oxon, OX14 4RN

Routledge is an imprint of the Taylor & Francis Group, an informa business

ISBN: 9781041349464 (hbk)
ISBN: 9781041349440 (pbk)
ISBN: 9781003795254 (ebk)

DOI: 10.4324/9781003795254

Typeset in Garamond
by Deanta Global Publishing Services, Chennai, India

To the healthcare professionals, Digital Health Experts and Consultants, and silent changemakers who strive daily to bridge the gap between care and technology, this book is dedicated to your efforts towards not only integrated but cognizant health. And to every patient whose well-being inspires innovation.

Contents

Disclaimer

The Core Interaction Model (CIM) is an independent framework developed by the author.

References to PMBOK® and PMI® are for comparative and educational purposes only. The author is not affiliated with or endorsed by the Project Management Institute.

Foreword

The digital transformation of healthcare is a present-day imperative. Across the globe, hospitals and health systems are embarking on complex journeys to implement sophisticated Health Information (HIS), with the dual promise of enhancing patient outcomes and achieving operational excellence. Yet, as many of us have witnessed, or even experienced firsthand, the path to a successful digital transition is littered with stalled projects, bloated budgets, and systems that, while technically sound, fail to win the hearts and minds of the clinicians they were built to serve.

In this critical landscape, the publication of Shahram Gharib's *Hospital Information System (HIS) Project Success: A Practical Guide in the Digital Era* is a timely and essential contribution. While I have not had the personal privilege of meeting the author, the insights contained within these pages speak to a profound, hard-won wisdom forged in the trenches of HIS implementation. This book moves beyond the "what" and "why" of digital health to confront the most pressing question: "How?"

At the heart of this guide lies the Core Interaction Model (CIM), a framework that represents a significant evolution in our approach to health information technology. For too long, health organizations have treated HIS implementations as mere technical projects, focusing on the installation of software and hardware. This outdated mindset is the root cause of countless failures. Mr Gharib correctly reframes these initiatives as profound organizational transformations, where technology is only one part of a much larger, human-centric equation.

The strength of the CIM is its inherent recognition that success is not a destination reached at go-live, but a continuous state achieved through a dynamic cycle of Observation, Implementation, and Qualification. CIM focuses on continuous feedback and real-world adaptation that makes the model so powerful.

In an era where artificial intelligence and predictive analytics are poised to revolutionize care, the principles embedded in the CIM become even more critical. AI models are not magical oracles; they are dependent on high-quality, contextualized data and seamless integration into clinical workflows. A poorly implemented HIS, one that is resisted by users and fails to capture accurate data, will starve even the most advanced AI of its lifeblood and render its insights unreliable or even dangerous.

The CIM, therefore, is more than a project management tool; it is the essential foundation for a future-proof, intelligent health system. Its emphasis on user-centered design ensures that technology augments rather than obstructs the work of healthcare professionals. By engaging clinicians, nurses, and administrative staff as active co-creators throughout the process, not just as end-users handed a finished product, the CIM builds the trust and ownership that are prerequisites for adoption and meaningful use.

As the world stands on the brink of a new age defined by AI-driven diagnostics, personalized medicine, and connected care, the lessons in this book are not merely helpful; they are foundational.

For leaders, practitioners, or visionaries committed to making digital health work for people, both those who provide care and those who receive it, this book is an essential guide. It provides the mindset, model, and practical steps to navigate the complexities of the digital health era and finally close the frustrating gap between technological potential and tangible, real-world success.

Saif Khairat, PhD, MPH, FACMI
Professor,
University of North Carolina at Chapel Hill

The views expressed in this foreword are my own and do not represent the positions of the University of North Carolina at Chapel Hill. This foreword does not imply endorsement of the entire volume by UNC-Chapel Hill or by me beyond this contribution.

Foreword

When I first entered the world of health informatics in the 1970s, I was driven by a simple yet profound conviction: That technology could fundamentally enhance the way we care for patients. Back then, many of my colleagues viewed computers in healthcare with skepticism, if not outright fear. I remember heated debates about whether technology would dehumanize medicine, whether nurses and doctors would lose the personal touch that defines quality care. Today, having spent over four decades in this field, I can say with certainty that when implemented thoughtfully, technology doesn't replace the human element – it amplifies our capacity to be better healthcare providers.

Shahram Gharib's *Hospital Information System (HIS) Project Success: A Practical Guide in the Digital Era* arrives at a pivotal moment in the digital transformation of healthcare. The challenges we face today are fundamentally different from those of the early days of health informatics. We are no longer asking whether technology can improve healthcare outcomes, but rather how we can most effectively and efficiently implement, integrate, and optimize these robust systems to serve patients, providers, and communities.

I've had the privilege of witnessing countless HIS implementations throughout my career – some triumphant, others cautionary tales. What I've learned is that technology alone never determines success. It's the people who make the difference. I've seen brilliant systems fail because they ignored the nurse who works the night shift. I've watched modest technologies transform entire hospitals because they were implemented with deep respect for the daily realities of caregivers and patients.

When I reflect on my journey from those early days of punch cards and mainframes to today's interconnected, AI-enhanced systems, I'm struck by how much the fundamental questions have evolved. We've moved from asking "Can technology help?" to "How do we ensure technology serves humanity effectively and also efficiently?" This shift represents not just technological progress but a maturation of our understanding of what healthcare transformation truly means.

What gives me hope about Shahram's approach is his recognition that successful HIS implementation is fundamentally about people and relationships. His emphasis on stakeholder engagement reminds me of a lesson I learned early in my career: The most sophisticated system is worthless if the people who must use it every day weren't part of designing it. I've spent years advocating for user-centered design in healthcare, and I see that philosophy woven throughout this guide.

The author's focus on cultural transformation particularly resonates with me. Over the decades, I've learned that changing technology is the easy part; changing culture is where the real work happens. I've seen organizations invest millions in state-of-the-art systems only to watch them fail because they underestimated the human dimension of change. This book doesn't make that mistake.

For those embarking on HIS projects – whether in traditional hospital settings or emerging care delivery models – this guide offers both strategic insight and practical wisdom. It acknowledges that success requires more than technical expertise; it demands leadership, vision, and an unwavering commitment to improving patient care through thoughtful technology implementation.

The future of healthcare depends on our ability to harness information systems not as ends in themselves, but as powerful tools in service of our highest calling: Healing and caring for those who need us most. This book provides the guidance necessary to achieve that noble goal.

Marion J. Ball, EdD, FACMI, FAAN, FIAHSI, FAHIMA, FMLA, FLHIMSS, FCHIME, FIMIA
Raj and Indra Nooyi Endowed Distinguished Chair in Bioengineering
Presidential Distinguished Professor and Executive Director
Center for Innovation in Health Informatics (CIHI)
University of Texas at Arlington

Preface

At 10:30 in the morning on a regular working day, I was summoned to the office of the Deputy for Specialized Hospital Services. The deputy was reviewing and signing some letters, while the project manager of the electronic health record (EHR) system was sitting in a chair in front of the deputy's desk.

As soon as I entered, the project manager gave me a look I'll never forget, and the deputy, without looking at me or even asking me to sit down, quickly asked a question, whose answer, and its consequences, changed my professional life forever.

Before I tell you what the question was, let me briefly explain the status of the EHR system in the hospital. The system had been in operation for four years. It was essentially a dataset into which trained users would enter patient treatment data by abstracting from paper records. This dataset was designed as a data tree (parent/child structure), with all information structured. After patient visits, trained users would read the notes written on paper forms and mark the relevant data items in the software. You might not agree with calling this software an "electronic health record", but that's what they were calling it, even in the contract. Though I agree with you that it was essentially a data repository with advanced search features and was not used by clinicians either.

In three years of operation, increasing complaints from medical staff led the deputy to pressure the project manager to enable the creation of parameterized electronic documents within the software. A year of effort led to nothing more than integrating some commercially available form builders into the software to place parameterized electronic documents on top of the dataset, with predictable consequences. Complaints increased. In every meeting and private conversation, the medical staff continued to criticize the software, and the deputy himself appeared overwhelmed.

As the only EHR expert in that hospital, responsible for software implementation and maintenance, I was under the most pressure, since all complaints eventually included me as well.

The project manager was also the CEO of the software company. He had come to the deputy to ask for overdue payments. I don't know what conversation happened before I entered that office, but from the deputy's tone and the way he asked the question, it didn't seem like a pleasant talk.

The project manager was a solo entrepreneur who seemed to have set up the company mainly to get projects officially. Until that day, the company had no more than four staff members, who had to handle all sales, marketing, planning, coordination, and system development tasks.

On the other hand, the total budget for that project at the time of contract signing was approximately $80,000 to be paid over five years. It's not hard to guess the outcome of a low-budget project that could barely cover the costs. It seemed the moment of facing failure had arrived.

The question I was asked was:

"Were you able to design the electronic documents in a way that is satisfying to the clinical staff?"

The answer wasn't a simple yes or no. How could clinical staff, who had not actively participated in any stage of the software implementation, expect solutions that could meet their expectations and make them satisfied? How could a deputy, who only occasionally received inconsistent reports from users, truly understand any answer from me or others? How could a project manager, who came from across the country every few months offering updates, expect widespread satisfaction? And how could a young specialist, working 12 hours a day just to cover assigned tasks, be confident about any answer?

At that moment, I tried to point out some of the challenges instead of giving a direct yes or no, but the deputy repeated his question more sharply, saying he only expected a yes or no answer.

In software projects, especially complex Hospital Information System (HIS) implementations and operations, such binary answers will create more confusion and misguidance instead of clarity. I will explain why in this book. But I was just a 29-year-old specialist without the experience to firmly say that I would not give a yes or no answer, and that functionality or lack thereof, is everyone's responsibility.

Still, the word "no" came out of my mouth. That was the excuse the deputy had been waiting for, making all payments dependent on user satisfaction. And the CEO, enraged by this decision, canceled the entire contract. Apparently, the result everyone wanted, except me, had been achieved.

That moment stayed with me like a scar. It didn't just mark the end of a failed project; it marked the beginning of a long journey. I realized that I never wanted to be in such a vulnerable and unclear position again, and I didn't want anyone else, especially those who cared deeply about healthcare IT, to find themselves in that either.

Since that day, I have participated in many other HIS implementation and operation projects, some in government hospitals, some in the private sector, and some in specialized departments. I explored various project management models (PMBOK), methodologies (Agile, Scrum, Lean), operational frameworks (Microsoft Operation Framework - MOF), and quality methodology (Six Sigma). Each brought its own improvement. The more I experimented and gained experience, the better I became at managing risks, handling stakeholders, and delivering value.

But even with all that, one thing kept bothering me: There was always a gap between what the system delivered and what the users truly needed, between project completion and actual satisfaction, and between installation and transformation.

I knew I needed to build a framework, not just for myself but for anyone navigating the difficult terrain of HIS implementation. Something continuous, practical, and human-centered. Something that would bridge the clinical, operational, and technical worlds.

This experience might sound familiar to many of us who have been involved in software implementation projects in hospitals.

That's how the Core Interaction Model (CIM) was developed. It's not a radical reinvention of everything we know, but a practical evolution in HIS implementation and operation management. CIM is built on real-world experience, shaped by failures and small victories. It's a response to that moment in the deputy's office, and to many others like it that followed. The model integrates Observation, Implementation, and Qualification into an ongoing loop, focusing not just on deployment, but on transformation that matters, that is sustainable, agile, and inclusive of all stakeholders.

In this book, I will share how CIM emerged, how it works, and how it fills the critical gap in HIS projects, helping teams move beyond software deployment toward true digital transformation in healthcare.

NOTE:

Generative artificial intelligence tools, including ChatGPT (versions 4o and 5), were used during the preparation of this manuscript exclusively to support language refinement and clarity. These tools assisted with grammatical corrections, improvement of readability, and formatting of references in accordance with the AMA citation style.

AI tools were also used to facilitate literature navigation by helping locate relevant content within previously identified textbooks and scholarly materials after sources had been independently selected and reviewed by the author.

In addition, Semantic Scholar AI was used to assist in identifying and listing potentially relevant academic publications. All sources cited in this book were independently reviewed, verified, and selected by the author. The intellectual content, interpretations, analyses, and conclusions presented herein are solely those of the author.

Author

Helping hospitals move from systems to success, one project at a time.

Shahram Gharib is a Digital Health Strategist and Hospital Information Systems (HIS) senior consultant with more than two decades of hands-on experience leading transformation programs across the Middle East. With an academic foundation (Master's Degree) in Health Information Technology and deep operational knowledge of advanced HIS platforms, he focuses on enabling safe, scalable, and sustainable digital ecosystems for healthcare organizations.

His work spans the full digital transformation lifecycle, from strategy and roadmap development to HIS implementation, interoperability, data and digital governance, and post-go-live operational excellence. Shahram is dedicated to advancing digital maturity, guided by global frameworks such as EMRAM and AMAM, while adapting these standards to regional realities and organizational culture.

He is the creator of the Core Interaction Model (CIM)**,** a continuous performance and alignment framework designed to help hospitals achieve HIS implementation and operational success by integrating observation, implementation, and qualification into an iterative, learning-oriented cycle. CIM reflects his core belief that technology must serve people, empower teams, and improve the lived experience of clinicians, patients, and administrators.

As an active member of the HIMSS Middle East Committee, Shahram contributes to knowledge exchange and capability development across health systems, ministries, and academic networks. His consultancy focus includes Digital Health Strategy, Data and Digital Governance, EMR Adoption, Digital Transformation Excellence, and Digital Health Workforce Capability Building**,** supporting organizations striving toward smarter care environments.

Beyond his professional life, Shahram enjoys writing, practicing Qigong, and spending time with family. His mission is simple yet ambitious: To help hospitals not only go digital but also go cognizant with clarity, confidence, and purpose.

Acknowledgments

Writing this book has been a journey of dedication, reflection, and learning, and I owe my deepest gratitude to those who supported me throughout the process. First and foremost, I would like to thank my family for their unwavering patience, love, and encouragement, especially during the moments when time and energy were scarce. Your belief in me gave me the strength to keep going. I am also grateful to my mentors and colleagues who shared their wisdom and insight, helping me shape my thoughts and sharpen the focus of this work.

To the readers and professionals who inspired the content of this book through their questions, challenges, and real-world experiences, thank you. You reminded me of the importance of staying grounded in practice while thinking forward. I also want to acknowledge the silent hours of solitude, the early mornings and late nights, which became the quiet companions of this endeavor. This book is as much yours as it is mine, and I hope it serves you well.

Chapter 1

Introduction

Digital transformation in healthcare is described as a fundamental, ongoing strategic shift driven by technology adoption to improve delivery and outcomes[1]. Digital transformation of healthcare can be disruptive; however, technologies such as the Internet of things, virtual care, remote monitoring, artificial intelligence, big data analytics, blockchain, smart wearables, platforms, tools enabling data exchange and storage, and tools enabling remote data capture and the exchange of data and sharing of relevant information across the health ecosystem creating a continuum of care have proven potential to enhance health outcomes by improving medical diagnosis, data-based treatment decisions, digital therapeutics, clinical trials, self-management of care, and person-centered care as well as creating more evidence-based knowledge, skills, and competence for professionals to support healthcare. Digital health is understood to mean "the field of knowledge and practice associated with the development and use of digital technologies to improve health"[2].

Digital transformation within the healthcare sector has progressed from being a forward-looking concept to becoming an essential requirement. This book examines one of the most significant drivers of this transformation: The Hospital Information System (HIS) projects.

As healthcare organizations continue to pursue better clinical outcomes, greater operational efficiency, and enhanced patient engagement, the implementation of HIS has become a fundamental component of their strategies. Studies report high rates of digital transformation initiatives failing due to technical, organizational, cultural, and interoperability challenges, including HIS projects[3].

DOI: 10.4324/9781003795254-1

This guide is intended for individuals actively involved in the implementation and operation of the Hospital Information System (HIS). It addresses the needs of IT professionals, consultants, hospital administrators, and clinical stakeholders.

Based on two decades of practical experience in both public and private healthcare settings, this book provides a comprehensive perspective. It integrates technical, organizational, and human considerations to support effective HIS project management and execution.

The Core Interaction Model (CIM) serves as both a conceptual and practical framework designed to transform the management and operation of Health Information System (HIS) projects. By integrating observation, implementation, and qualification into a continuous cycle, CIM moves beyond conventional project phases. This approach supports seamless collaboration, adaptability, and a focus on performance-based outcomes.

The book unfolds in a structured manner:

Chapter 1 introduces the context, challenges, and evolving expectations in healthcare IT, tracing how Hospital Information System (HIS) has matured and why it is indispensable today.

Chapter 2 presents the Core Interaction Model, its structure, and its alignment with standard project management practices.

Chapter 3 translates theory into practice, showcasing principles and actionable strategies for continuous stakeholder engagement, adaptive delivery, system usability, and long-term success.

Chapter 4 focuses on HIS project success in the smart future healthcare ecosystem.

Whether you are starting a new Hospital Information System (HIS) project, addressing challenges in an existing implementation, or seeking to enhance an operational system, this book provides more than solutions. It introduces a perspective rooted in continuous improvement, user empathy, and strategic alignment.

Begin the process of making HIS projects not only effective but also transformative.

Healthcare IT Advances Comparing to Other Industries

Hospital Information System (HIS) has substantially evolved over recent decades, forming the foundation of modern digital health[4]. Despite the efforts, the pace of technological advancement in healthcare has not matched that of industries such as finance or retail. Several factors have contributed to this slower rate of adoption. The complexity of healthcare data, stringent regulatory requirements, and the high standards necessary to ensure patient safety have all played significant roles in shaping the industry's approach to technology.

Nevertheless, there have been considerable achievements in specific areas, including artificial intelligence, telehealth, and cloud computing. These advancements demonstrate the sector's capacity for innovation when conditions allow.

Looking ahead, the primary challenge lies in accelerating the integration of advanced technologies while upholding the privacy and security standards essential to patient care. Research discusses future challenges in digital health, including security, privacy, and integration of advanced IT[5].

The development of Information Technology (IT) within the healthcare sector reflects a continuous progression of innovations designed to address the increasing complexity of patient care, administrative processes, and medical research. The following timeline highlights significant milestones in the adoption and advancement of IT in healthcare.

1950s–1960s: The Early Days of Healthcare IT

Historical surveys note that the earliest computer applications in large hospital settings focused on administrative processing[6]. The first use of computers in healthcare began in the 1950s, primarily for administrative tasks like payroll and accounting. Hospitals adopted mainframe computers, which were large, expensive, and mainly used for record-keeping.

In the early 1960s, healthcare facilities began using the early Hospital Information System (HIS). The Lockheed Corporation developed the first comprehensive HIS in 1965, known as Technicon Medical Information System (TMIS), for El Camino Hospital in California. This system handled both administrative and clinical information.

Laboratory Information System (LIS) and Billing System also emerged, focused on automating lab test management and patient billing processes.

1970s: Growth of Clinical Applications

Medical informatics histories describe initial EMR concepts emerging in the 1970s alongside HIS developments[7]. Early systems were limited to specific tasks like storing lab results or patient histories.
In 1971, the US National Library of Medicine introduced MEDLINE, a pioneering medical database, allowing healthcare professionals to access a wide range of medical research articles.
Development of Standards: During this time, the need for data standardization was recognized, and organizations like ASTM International began developing standards for healthcare IT.

1980s: The Birth of Modern HIS

Comprehensive, department-spanning HIS architectures emerged in the 1980s, integrating administrative and clinical functions[8]. This included patient demographics, clinical data, and imaging records.
The VistA System: In 1983, the US Department of Veterans Affairs implemented the VistA (Veterans Health Information Systems and Technology Architecture) system, a comprehensive HIS that included early forms of electronic health records.
Computerized Provider Order Entry (CPOE) emerged in the 1980s–1990s and demonstrated reductions in medication errors[9].
PACS development and early clinical deployment began in the early-mid 1980s[10], allowing digital storage and sharing of medical imaging, significantly improving access to diagnostic tools.

1990s: Wider Adoption and Integration

Multiple adoption studies confirm slow diffusion of EHRs pre-2000 due to cost and organizational barriers[11].
HL7 was established in 1987 but gained prominence in the 1990s. HL7 is a set of international standards for transferring clinical and administrative data between software applications in healthcare.
Telemedicine pilot programs and video-based consultations expanded during the 1990s[12]. This laid the foundation for the broader telehealth services we see today.
Industry histories and informatics reviews document vendor emergence and market consolidation in the 1990s.

2000s: Policy and Technological Expansion

In the US, the Health Information Technology for Economic and Clinical Health (HITECH) Act of 2009 incentivized hospitals and physicians to adopt EHRs by offering financial rewards for "meaningful use" of these systems.

Efforts to ensure that different healthcare systems could share patient data effectively across facilities increased, focusing on interoperability. Regional and national health information exchanges were developed to facilitate this process.

Patients began to take a more active role in managing their health data through personal health records (PHRs), which allowed them to store and access their health information online.

2010s: Digital Health and Advanced Technologies

With the widespread adoption of EHRs, the focus shifted toward leveraging health data for predictive analytics, population health management, and personalized medicine.

Clinical decision support, imaging diagnostics, and predictive modeling literature expanded significantly after 2010[13].

The rise of smartphones and wearable technology transformed how patients interacted with their health data. mHealth apps enabled remote monitoring, telemedicine consultations, and better chronic disease management.

With the increasing volume of sensitive health data being stored and transferred electronically, cybersecurity has become a critical issue. Blockchain in health is mostly exploratory and conceptual; your wording "explored" is correct and safe[14].

2020s: Digital Transformation and Pandemic Response

The novel coronavirus disease-19 (COVID-19) pandemic has altered our economy, society, and healthcare system[15]. Telemedicine became the norm for remote consultations, and health information systems were essential in tracking the virus, managing vaccines, and coordinating care.

The integration of AI into genomics allowed for more sophisticated analysis of genetic data, opening up new possibilities in personalized medicine, particularly in areas like cancer treatment and rare disease diagnostics.

Cloud-based health information systems became more popular, offering scalability and flexibility in managing large amounts of health data while ensuring accessibility across multiple healthcare settings.

The use of connected devices, such as wearables and remote patient monitoring systems, has increased significantly, enhancing the ability of healthcare providers to monitor patients outside traditional care settings.

Foundational informatics literature describing heterogeneous data types (clinical text, imaging, and genomics) and privacy sensitivity[8]. It includes a wide range of information such as clinical notes, diagnostic results, medical images, and procedural reports. Studies documenting fragmented HIS/EHR landscapes and siloed architectures[16]. Empirical evaluations of HL7/FHIR adoption show uneven implementation and limited real-world interoperability[17]. This situation presents considerable obstacles for professionals working in digital health.

Regulatory frameworks like HIPAA and GDPR are designed to safeguard privacy and security. However, these regulations can also impede innovation and are sometimes cited as reasons for delaying technological progress. While it is essential to address concerns related to patient safety and data confidentiality, the healthcare industry continues to require increased investment, innovation, and collaboration to drive meaningful advancement.

In addition to technical obstacles, the healthcare sector contends with significant financial burdens, fragmented operational environments, and notable resistance to organizational change. Many hospitals, particularly those outside of affluent regions, lack the resources to invest in modern, standardized Hospital Information System (HIS) solutions. As a result, the adoption of these systems is often delayed, and implementation projects frequently encounter setbacks or fail to achieve their objectives.

Studies on clinician burnout, change fatigue, and health IT adoption resistance[18]. These conditions reduce their willingness to adapt to new workflows introduced by technological advancements. In contrast to sectors such as banking, where all parties benefit from comprehensive digital documentation, stakeholders in healthcare often have divergent priorities. This misalignment increases complexity and poses additional barriers to successful system adoption.

Furthermore, the sector's inherent caution and the necessity for thorough validation processes contribute to a slower pace of modernization. These factors collectively impede the widespread implementation of the advanced Hospital Information System (HIS).

Comparative analytics literature showing early healthcare adoption in research and insurance[19]. The use of data-driven analysis was rapidly embraced in scientific research and by insurance companies, resulting in improved speed and accuracy in decision-making processes.

While the application of big data for population health management and patient outcomes is still evolving, the healthcare sector continues to advance alongside other fields. Artificial intelligence and machine learning have supported a range of functions, including medical image analysis, genomic modeling, and operational forecasting, well before the emergence of generative AI and chatbots. This history underscores healthcare's early and sustained engagement with advanced technological solutions.

During the COVID-19 pandemic, telehealth, remote care, and consumer-centered innovations experienced significant acceleration, fundamentally altering expectations for healthcare delivery. The widespread adoption of virtual clinics and remote services was driven by both political support and public demand. As a result, the role of the IT department evolved from a peripheral function to a strategic component at the core of hospital operations.

Patients now anticipate a level of convenience in healthcare comparable to what they encounter in banking and retail, including mobile access, online portals, and digital payment options. In response, healthcare organizations are investing in technologies such as wearables, Internet of Things (IoT) devices, and remote monitoring systems. These advancements not only facilitate preventive care but also signify a broader transition toward digital, accessible, and patient-centered healthcare.

Healthcare has consistently been at the forefront of technological advancement, particularly in the areas of medical imaging, robotics, and genomics. Imaging technologies such as X-ray, MRI, and CT have established global benchmarks for precision. These innovations have not only transformed medical diagnostics but have also influenced progress in sectors like aerospace and defense. Notably, early applications of machine learning in image analysis achieved significant accuracy well before artificial intelligence became widely adopted.

Robotic surgery has further extended the boundaries of precision and safety in medical procedures, demonstrating the sector's commitment to rigorous standards. In addition, significant developments in genomics, including cloning, gene sequencing, and personalized medicine, have advanced the capabilities of data analysis and algorithmic interpretation. As a result, healthcare remains ahead of many other industries in the ability to interpret and apply complex genetic information.

Progress in a Hospital Information System (HIS) is often hindered by the lack of standardized operational workflows within clinical care. The delivery of healthcare is complex and subject to considerable variability, with processes differing not only among providers and specialities but also between individual patient cases. This variability creates significant challenges in designing systems that can accommodate diverse requirements without substantial customization.

In contrast to industries with more predictable and uniform workflows, healthcare must address both clinical variability and stringent safety standards. These factors contribute to the slower adoption of standardized digital solutions across the sector.

Furthermore, the high degree of customization necessary during the implementation of HIS and Electronic Health Record (EHR) systems leads to increased deployment times and costs. Adapting these platforms to align with local workflows demands significant stakeholder involvement, which can further delay system implementation and limit the scalability of digital transformation within healthcare.

HIS Is Revolutionizing Healthcare

Healthcare delivery has historically focused on episodic, symptom-driven care rather than continuous prevention[20]. When individuals experience symptoms, they consult a physician, and the primary focus centers on identifying the underlying cause to establish a diagnosis and determine an appropriate treatment plan.

However, the shift from reactive treatment to preventive, value-based, and population-oriented care is widely documented[21]. This evolution aims to enhance not only the quality of treatment but also the overall patient experience within the healthcare system.

To support this shift, there is a clear need for tools that facilitate faster and more informed clinical decision-making. Such tools should address several key objectives:

- Reducing human errors and minimizing unnecessary duplication of tests.

- Enhancing continuity of care across different providers and settings.
- Providing timely alerts for drug-drug interactions and abnormal laboratory values.
- Offering access to predictive analytics for improved clinical outcomes.
- Improving patient throughput and reducing wait times.
- Decreasing administrative burdens for healthcare professionals.
- Extending care beyond the traditional boundaries of hospitals.
- Supporting the development of individualized treatment plans.
- Ensuring access to comprehensive, lifetime health and disease data for each patient.

However, it is important to recognize that the true catalyst for progress in healthcare lies not solely in the tools themselves, but in the discoveries made by some of the most intelligent individuals throughout history. These discoveries, along with the instruments developed to reveal, document, and advance them, have consistently shaped the evolution of medical practice.

This pattern of progress is not unprecedented. Since the era of Hippocrates, often regarded as the Father of Medicine, who advocated for understanding diseases as natural phenomena rather than supernatural occurrences, the field of healthcare has experienced several major revolutions. These range from the introduction of clinical observation into medical practice to the development of mRNA vaccines in the modern era.

Health data management is a core responsibility of healthcare organizations due to its direct impact on patient safety, quality of care, and organizational performance[8]. Errors, delays, or miscommunication can have serious consequences. Real-time electronic access to patient data improves safety, coordination, and clinical decision-making[22]. Without such systems, healthcare professionals would still rely on paper records, manual files, and phone calls to access essential data.

Integrated HIS architectures enable interdepartmental communication and coordination of clinical services[23]. This integration streamlines workflows and enables healthcare providers to deliver more efficient and timely care. Additionally, HIS assists in managing hospital resources such as beds, staff, and supplies, which contributes to both operational efficiency and cost savings.

Another significant benefit of HIS is its support for organizational planning and informed decision-making. Electronic health data are widely used for quality measurement, compliance audits, and public health surveillance[24]. Furthermore, HIS offers predictive insights that aid in preparing for emergencies and anticipating future trends, allowing healthcare institutions to move from reactive to proactive management (Figure 1.1).

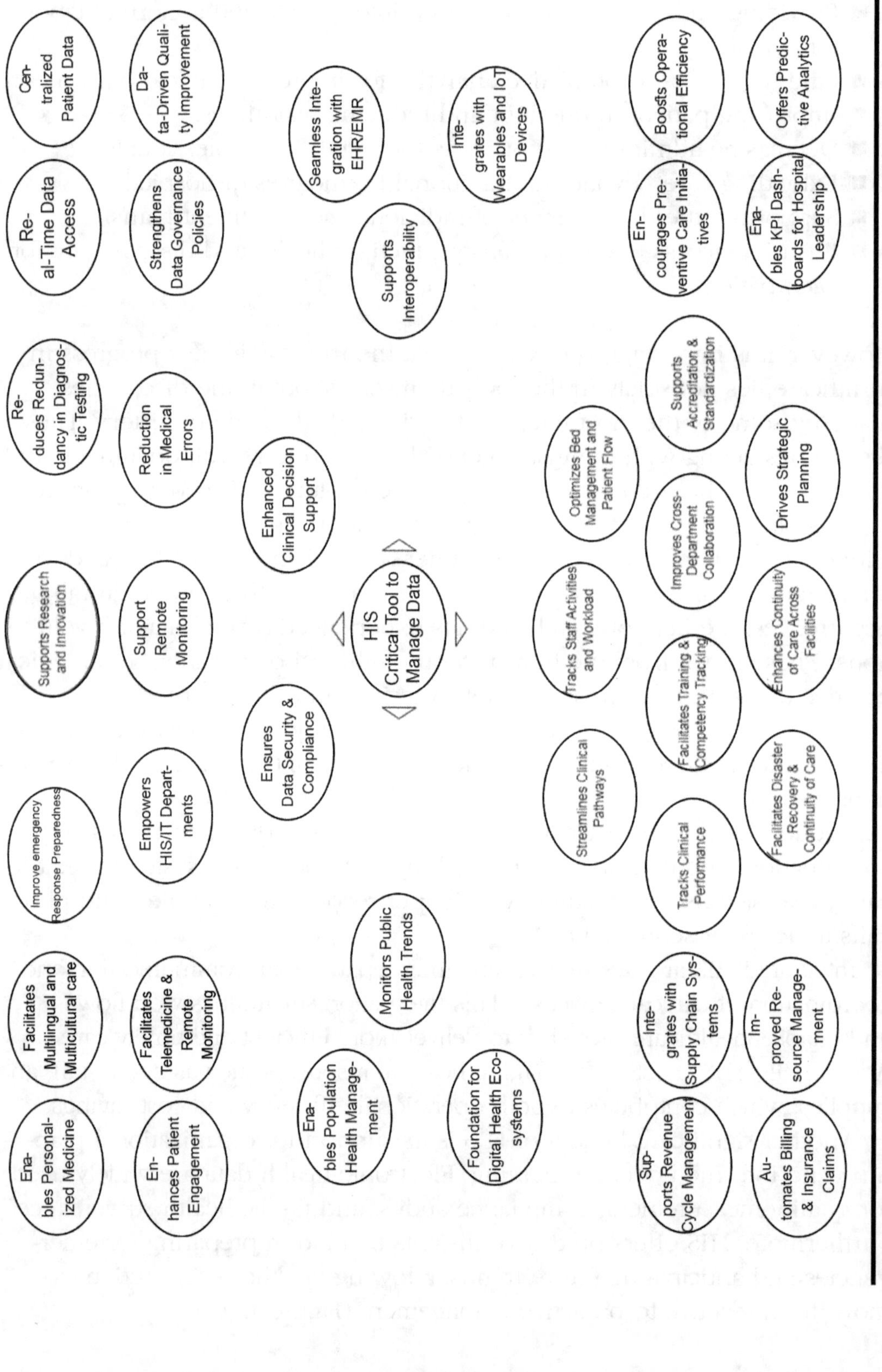

Figure 1.1 HIS – The Backbone of Modern Health Data Management

Defining the HIS Scope: What Every Project Must Support

The evolution of medical and information technologies over the last two centuries has fundamentally transformed data collection, documentation, and analysis in healthcare[25]. These advancements have enabled the creation of more effective and practical solutions for collecting, sharing, and processing medical information, capabilities that were unimaginable to previous generations. One of the most notable innovations in this area is the Hospital Information System (HIS).

A Hospital Information System (HIS) also promotes effective teamwork among nurses, physicians, and administrative staff by ensuring that all parties have access to the same information. This collaborative environment improves communication and enables better patient care. Electronic records and patient-facing systems support engagement and shared decision-making[26]. Ultimately, while HIS is a technological system, its greatest value lies in fostering closer connections among individuals, teams, departments, and entire healthcare organizations (Table 1.1).

A modern Hospital Information System (HIS) functions as an integrated platform supporting clinical, administrative, and strategic processes[27]. Today, they serve as the foundation for modern healthcare delivery, supporting decision-making processes and fostering collaboration among care teams. The development of these systems reflects the increasing expectations placed on digital health, including the enhancement of patient care, the advancement of personalized medicine, and the empowerment of healthcare professionals.

Despite their significance and advanced capabilities, establishing a functional and effective HIS remains a complex undertaking. Numerous hospitals continue to encounter difficulties such as unsuccessful implementations, limited user adoption, or systems that fail to address the practical needs of their users. The central issue has shifted from questioning the necessity of HIS to determining how to implement and operate these systems successfully.

The challenge of demonstrating the value of healthcare information technology is not new. Historically, it required extensive advocacy, research, and persistent effort. Currently, the focus has moved away from justifying the adoption of technology toward ensuring its effective integration within healthcare organizations. Achieving this integration depends not only on the technical systems themselves but also on engaging stakeholders, managing complexity, and providing purposeful leadership.

Table 1.1 Main Functional Features of a Modern HIS, Matrix Aligned with Digital Maturity

Maturity Stage	**Functional Domain**	**Core Capabilities**
Foundational	Administrative and Operational Systems	Patient registration, admission/discharge, billing, scheduling, HR, inventory, and basic reporting
	Clinical Information Management	Basic EMR/EHR functionality, structured documentation, diagnosis coding, and medication lists
	Security and Compliance	Role-based access, basic encryption, data backups, and audit logs
Developing	Diagnostic and Treatment Systems	Integration with LIS, RIS, PACS, PIS; automated test orders and results; lab and imaging workflow
	Decision Support	Rule-based clinical alerts, care plan templates, allergy and interaction warnings
	Resource Management	Asset tracking, staff scheduling, and room/equipment utilization
Established	Communication and Interoperability	HL7/FHIR-based integration, health information exchange (HIE), e-referrals, and internal system communication
	Analytics and Reporting	Real-time dashboards, clinical quality indicators, and operational analytics
	Patient and Provider Communication	Patient portals, e-consent, appointment reminders, and secure messaging
Advanced	Decision Support and Intelligence	Predictive analytics, AI-driven clinical decision support, risk stratification
	Patient Engagement and Remote Monitoring	Mobile health apps, wearable integration, and remote patient monitoring (RPM)
	Personalized and Proactive Care	Tailored patient education, behavior tracking, and care gap alerts
	Data Governance and Strategy	Enterprise data strategy, federated data architecture, and automated compliance reporting

The subsequent chapter addresses the practical aspects of bringing an HIS to life within a hospital setting. It examines the factors that contribute to the success or failure of such projects, strategies for overcoming organizational resistance, and the limitations of traditional project management approaches in the healthcare context. In addition, it introduces the Core Interaction Model (CIM), a healthcare-specific framework developed over two decades of experience with HIS projects. This model is intended to align implementation and operational processes, supporting ongoing performance, engagement, and adaptability in real-world hospital environments.

While the first chapter established the importance of HIS, the following chapter will focus on practical methods for ensuring its effective, sustainable, and collaborative use.

References

1. Stoumpos AI, Kitsios F, Talias MA. Digital transformation in healthcare: Technology acceptance and its applications. *Int J Environ Res Public Health.* 2023 Feb 15;20(4):13407. doi:10.3390/ijerph20043407
2. *Global Strategy on Digital Health 2020–2027.* Geneva, Switzerland: World Health Organization; 2025. Accessed January 3, 2026. https://iris.who.int/server/api/core/bitstreams/a64d584f-015b-471f-9d86-9ea263cfb516/content
3. Hundal GS, Rhodes D, Laux C. Digital transformation of healthcare enterprises in the era of disruptions—a structured literature review. *Sustainability.* 2025; 17(13):35690. https://doi.org/10.3390/su17135690
4. Shen Y, Yu J, Zhou J, Hu G. Twenty-Five years of evolution and hurdles in electronic health records and interoperability in medical research: Comprehensive review. *J Med Internet Res.* 2025;27:e59024. Published January 9, 42025. doi:10.2196/59024
5. Sinha R. The role and impact of new technologies on healthcare systems. *Discover Health Syst.* 2024;3:96.
6. Collen MF, Miller RA. The early history of hospital information systems for inpatient care in the United States. In: Lehmann CU, Ammenwerth E, Nøhr C, eds. *Health Information Systems: Architectures and Strategies.* Springer; 2015. doi:10.1007/978-1-4471-6732-7_6
7. Shen Y, Yu J, Zhou J, Hu G. Twenty-five years of evolution and hurdles in electronic health records and interoperability in medical research: comprehensive review. *J Med Internet Res.* 2025 Jan 9;27:e59024. doi:10.2196/59024
8. Haux R. Health information systems - past, present, future. *Int J Med Inform.* 2006;75(3–4):268–281.
9. Evans RS, et al. A computerized order entry system for medications and laboratory tests. *JAMA.* 1998;280(15):1311–1316.

10. Huang HK. *PACS and Imaging Informatics: Basic Principles and Applications.* Hoboken, NJ: Wiley-Blackwell; 2010.
11. McCullough JS. The adoption of hospital information systems. *Health Econ.* 2008;17(5):649–11664. doi:10.1002/hec.1283
12. Bashshur RL, Shannon GW, Smith BR, et al. The empirical foundations of telemedicine interventions for chronic disease management. *Telemed J E Health.* 2014;20(9):769–12800. doi:10.1089/tmj.2014.9981
13. Shickel B, Tighe PJ, Bihorac A, Rashidi P. Deep EHR: A survey of recent advances in deep learning techniques for Electronic Health Record (EHR) analysis. *IEEE J Biomed Health Inform.* 2018;22(5):1589–131604. doi:10.1109/JBHI.2017.2767063
14. Kuo TT, Kim HE, Ohno-Machado L. Blockchain distributed ledger technologies for biomedical and healthcare applications. *J Am Med Inform Assoc.* 2017;24(6):1211–141220. doi:10.1093/jamia/ocx068
15. Wosik J, Fudim M, Cameron B, et al. Telehealth transformation: COVID-19 and the rise of virtual care. *J Am Med Inform Assoc.* 2020;27(6):957–15962. doi:10.1093/jamia/ocaa067
16. Adler-Milstein J, Everson J, Lee SY. EHR adoption and hospital performance: Time-related effects. *Health Serv Res.* 2015;50(6):1751–161771. doi:10.1111/1475–6773.12406
17. Mandel JC, Kreda DA, Mandl KD, Kohane IS, Ramoni RB. SMART on FHIR: A standards-based, interoperable apps platform for electronic health records. *J Am Med Inform Assoc.* 2016;23(5):899–17908. doi:10.1093/jamia/ocv189
18. Carayon P, et al. Health IT and clinician workload. *BMJ Qual Saf.* 2015;24(1):84–94.
19. Topol EJ. High-performance medicine: The convergence of human and artificial intelligence. *Nat Med.* 2019;25(1):44–1956. doi:10.1038/s41591-018-0300-7
20. Porter ME, Teisberg EO. *Redefining HealthCare.* Boston, MA: Harvard Business School Press; 2006.
21. Bodenheimer T, Berry-Millett R. Care management of patients with complex health needs. *Ann Fam Med.* 2009;7(5):404–411.
22. Bates DW, Gawande AA. Improving safety with information technology. *N Engl J Med.* 2003;348(25):2526–2534.
23. Winter A, et al. Health information systems architecture. *Health Inf Sci Syst.* 2013;1:2.
24. Adler-Milstein J, et al. EHR data for quality and reporting. *Health Aff.* 2017;36(7):1218–1225.
25. Bynum WF. *Science and the Practice of Medicine in the Nineteenth Century.* Cambridge University Press; 1994.
26. Kruse CS, et al. Patient portals and engagement. *J Med Internet Res.* 2015;17(6):e148.
27. Menachemi N, Collum TH. Benefits and drawbacks of EHR systems. *Risk Manag Healthc Policy.* 2011;4:47–55.

Chapter 2

HIS Implementation and Operational Excellence

Digital transformation in hospitals delivers value but introduces technical, organizational, and financial challenges. Successful digital transformation initiatives, for example, digital twins for supply chains, augmented reality, the IoT, and cybersecurity technology initiatives, implemented significantly enhanced resiliency in supply chain and manufacturing operations. However, according to another study conducted by McKinsey & Company, 70% of digital transformation efforts for healthcare enterprises fail to meet their goals. Healthcare enterprises face unique challenges, such as complex regulatory environments, cultural resistance, workforce IT skills, and the need for data interoperability, which make digital transformation a challenging project[1]. Health IT and HIS implementations require high upfront and ongoing investment, particularly for infrastructure, licensing, and change management[2]. In addition, resistance to change among clinicians and staff is a well-documented barrier to HIS and EHR adoption[3]. Other common obstacles include interoperability and standardization issues, cybersecurity concerns, insufficient training and support, technical and infrastructure limitations, and challenges related to data quality and governance. These factors can significantly impede progress.

Given the complexity and variety of these challenges, the implementation of a Hospital Information System (HIS) requires a structured project management approach. Such an approach enables comprehensive planning to address technical, human, and organizational factors in a systematic manner. It also facilitates effective resource allocation, ensuring that financial, human,

DOI: 10.4324/9781003795254-2

and technological resources are appropriately distributed. Risk management is essential for identifying potential risks early and developing suitable mitigation strategies. Engaging stakeholders, including clinicians, IT professionals, and administrators, promotes communication and collaboration across disciplines. Furthermore, ongoing monitoring and evaluation allow for the establishment of metrics to assess progress, quality, and outcomes, supporting continuous improvement.

A systematic literature review by Soe Ye Yint Tun and Samaneh Madanian, published in JAMIA in 2023, identified project management as one of the most critical success factors in the implementation of Clinical Information Systems[4]. Without a well-structured project framework, many of the aforementioned challenges tend to arise and intensify over time. The complexity of healthcare workflows, combined with resistance to change, can exacerbate these difficulties and create an environment where progress is hindered.

Health IT challenges often evolve into systemic organizational problems when governance, structure, and alignment are lacking[5]. Lack of formal project structure and governance increases the likelihood of failure in HIS initiatives[6]. In the absence of the structure and support provided by a dedicated HIS project, most hospitals lack the strategic capacity, cross-functional collaboration, and resource planning necessary to address these issues effectively. As a result, organizations may become trapped in a cycle of inefficiency and risk, which can ultimately lead to the abandonment of the HIS initiative and the loss of invested effort and resources.

Many Hospital Information System (HIS) specialists have become accustomed to changing projects every two to four years. This practice often arises from the recognition that it is preferable to transition before significant challenges emerge, particularly when concerns about system performance begin to surface. Notably, most photographs documenting these projects are taken within the first year following system deployment, rather than in subsequent periods.

Information systems literature clearly distinguishes system development from organizational implementation[7]. HIS development is primarily concerned with designing and building the software, coding its features, and ensuring that the product is both functional and adaptable to a range of healthcare requirements. This phase is highly technical, focusing on creating a robust, scalable, and secure system.

In contrast, HIS implementation involves integrating the completed system into the specific environment of a healthcare organization. The emphasis shifts from software creation to adapting and deploying the system within the hospital's operational, technical, and clinical context.

HIS implementation is a complex, multidisciplinary process that extends beyond technical installation. It requires coordinated efforts among various stakeholders, including hospital management, clinicians, IT personnel, and vendors. The goal is to ensure that the system's functionality aligns with organizational workflows, regulatory standards, and clinical practices.

- Engaging stakeholders
- Mapping existing processes
- Conducting user training
- Managing data migration
- Overseeing change management
- Integrating with current infrastructure

These activities demand strong project management skills to address challenges such as resistance to change, potential downtime, and the need to secure user adoption.

HIS implementation is a dynamic, evolving process rather than a static deployment[8]. The process must accommodate the evolving needs of the healthcare organization while minimizing disruptions to patient care. Post-deployment optimization and iterative refinement are essential for sustained HIS effectiveness[9].

In summary, while HIS development produces the system, HIS implementation ensures that it is effectively utilized to achieve organizational objectives. Both phases are distinct and equally important.

To further clarify, consider a software company that develops an HIS. The development team's objective is to create a system capable of handling general tasks such as patient registration, billing, and medical record management. They establish a solid technical foundation, ensuring the software can be adapted to various hospitals. This development phase typically concludes when the software is ready for deployment. Implementation, however, begins at this point and focuses on applying the system to meet the unique needs of each hospital.

Hospital Information System (HIS) implementation occurs after the software has been developed and delivered to the hospital. This process involves deploying the system within the hospital environment and is often part of routine operations. The implementation team is responsible for configuring the system to align with the hospital's specific workflows.

For instance, the system must be tailored to accommodate the hospital's procedures for scheduling appointments, documenting and reviewing patient information, sending reminders to clinicians regarding the latest patient data, checking for drug-to-drug interactions, integrating with other systems and point-of-care devices, and managing billing codes. Effective implementation requires close collaboration with hospital staff to ensure that the software supports their daily activities.

Implementation extends beyond simply installing the system or creating master data. It involves adapting the software so that it functions seamlessly within the hospital's unique operational environment.

A useful analogy is the difference between building a car and learning to drive it. Developing an HIS is comparable to designing and constructing a car, ensuring all features are present and the vehicle is safe and functional. Implementing an HIS, however, is similar to modifying features and training an individual to drive that car in a particular city, with its own roads, traffic regulations, and challenges. Each hospital operates under its own set of workflows, regulations, and organizational culture. HIS implementation ensures that the system is customized to function effectively within these specific conditions.

NOTE:

Implementing and adapting a Hospital Information System (HIS) are not the same concept. This is because a Hospital Information System (HIS) is customized to the overall needs of an organization, and its implementation does not necessarily mean its use by end users.

The implementation of a Hospital Information System (HIS) requires a structured approach. The process typically begins with careful project planning, followed by experimental installation and formal acceptance. It is important to note that the process does not end with initial acceptance; ongoing efforts are necessary, as this stage marks the commencement of daily operations and user interaction with the system.

Several critical factors influence the successful deployment of an information system in a healthcare setting. Success is more likely in smaller organizations with less complex environments. Conversely, as organizational size and technological complexity increase, the risk of failure also rises.

- System Design: Systems that are not appropriately designed, such as those with inadequate performance in meeting user needs, can significantly hinder successful implementation.
- User and Human Factors: Even technically sound systems may fail if user needs and human factors are not adequately addressed.

Healthcare organizations often operate within intricate networks that encompass political, cultural, and technical dimensions. These complexities can create significant challenges during system customization. Furthermore, insufficient project management and a lack of attention to user experience during implementation may result in failure, even when the system functions correctly from a technical standpoint.

There are primary factors that significantly influence the implementation process in healthcare settings. Implementing a healthcare information system is inherently a dual process, involving both technological and organizational components. The interaction between these elements plays a critical role in determining the success of implementation efforts. Effective implementation requires the establishment of a comprehensive framework that supports users and manages system operations. Such a framework is essential for integrating the implementation process and providing a solid foundation for organizational transformation, which is crucial for long-term success. It is also necessary for healthcare information system management to maintain a balanced approach between organizational change and system design. This balance helps to prevent conflicts that may arise during the implementation phase.

With over two decades of experience in Healthcare Information Systems implementation and operations, I have encountered a wide range of challenges. Throughout this period, I have consistently sought effective solutions to address these issues. Although I experimented with various project management and operational models, none fully achieved seamless alignment between implementation and operations, sustained stakeholder engagement, or the integration of real-time performance monitoring, feedback, and adaptation. Additionally, common issues such as phase fragmentation and role confusion persisted in hospital environments.

In response to these challenges, I developed a new model specifically designed to address the unique requirements of Hospital Information System (HIS) implementation and operation.

Core Interaction Model in HIS Implementation and Operation

While the PMBOK framework offers a comprehensive set of principles and performance domains, its broad nature may not sufficiently address the complexities of highly specialized or multidimensional projects such as Hospital Information System (HIS) implementations. These projects often demand a more customized approach to manage their dynamic characteristics, multidisciplinary collaboration, and the significant stakes present in healthcare environments.

Health IT success depends on organizational assimilation and sustained use, not mere system delivery[8]. It involves integrating technology into an active healthcare system while minimizing disruption to patient care. Iterative, stakeholder-centric approaches are better suited to complex healthcare environments than rigid linear models[5]. This complexity necessitates project management models that prioritize ongoing stakeholder interaction, continuous progress, and adaptability to feedback from real-world use. Traditional methodologies, such as the waterfall model, may lack the required flexibility, and even agile frameworks may not fully address the operational and regulatory challenges unique to healthcare. Addressing these gaps is essential.

The Core Interaction Model emphasizes continuous implementation, observation, and qualification, ensuring that the system evolves in alignment with organizational needs while maintaining agility. This approach enables project teams to better integrate multidisciplinary inputs, manage resistance to change, and align technical solutions with clinical outcomes. As a result, there is a clear rationale for adopting project management models tailored to specific industries or project types, rather than relying solely on generalized frameworks.

Effective project management models are founded on several key principles, including:

- Careful planning
- Sustainable development
- Team building
- Risk reduction
- Change management
- Cost and time management
- Continuous feedback
- Product maintenance

Traditional information system development models often separate users (as feedback providers) from producers (as designers and implementers)[10]. In practice, users typically provide feedback, while producers manage the remaining processes. However, in complex projects such as HIS implementation, users play a more integral role. Lack of sustained user engagement is a major contributor to HIS and EHR implementation failure[11]. Without their active involvement throughout all stages, it is nearly impossible to achieve successful implementation while effectively managing costs, time, risks, and changes.

In hospital settings, users encompass a diverse group of staff with varying skills and backgrounds, including administrative, financial, medical, and IT personnel. Each group interacts with the software differently, and certain teams, such as IT, are particularly critical to the implementation process.

Agile and V-Model principles are commonly adapted and hybridized for complex, regulated systems[12]. The Core Interaction Model is an advanced approach derived from Agile and the V-Model. It places particular emphasis on requirement analysis and quality assurance during system implementation. Each enhancement within this model is supported by thorough analysis and quality assurance measures.

This model is specifically designed for HIS implementation and operation, involving software developers, hospital IT specialists, and end users as key participants in the process.

The Core Interaction Model prioritizes flexibility, incremental delivery, and continuous optimization. It also emphasizes ongoing collaboration among the development team, hospital IT staff, and end users to ensure comprehensive requirement analysis, software feature testing, and quality assurance.

Unlike traditional project management models that often follow a phase-driven structure, this model views projects as dynamic systems composed of interdependent elements: Observation, Implementation, and Qualification, all with a focus on performance. These elements work together to enhance performance, maintain agility, and seamlessly integrate both implementation and operational phases. Collectively, they form the core of the project and are central to its success.

This chapter introduces the foundational principles of the Core Interaction Model, outlines its distinctive features, and explains how it addresses the primary challenges associated with HIS implementation and operation.

The Core Interaction Model: A Conceptual Model

Inspired by the atomic structure, the Core Interaction Model views a project as a dynamic system composed of three fundamental "particles":

1. **Observation**: The element responsible for identifying needs, monitoring progress, and gathering insights. Observation serves as the "electron" of the project, providing agility and responsiveness to external and internal changes.
   a. Identifying Needs: Identifying all user and system requirements through IT and medical informatics experts working in the hospital. They are familiar with all processes, trusted by hospital staff, and can serve as a strong technical bridge between end users and software developers.
   b. Monitoring Progress: Monitoring progress in software feature development and following up on them.
   c. Gathering Insights: Receiving feedback from end users during acceptance testing to approve software features and usability.
   d. Functional Design and Configuration: Defining master data, maintaining system configuration, designing electronic forms and reports, and system logic design.
2. **Implementation:** Representing the "proton", Implementation forms the core of the project, driving execution and establishing the foundation for success. It involves resource allocation, task execution, and overall project structuring.
   a. Technical Analysis: Overall system architecture design, module design or redesign, interface design, and system logic.
   b. Development: Developing functionalities according to user needs and objectives.
   c. Technical Testing: Testing and reviewing the performance of each module individually and in relation to other modules and systems before the acceptance test.
3. **Qualification:** As the "neutron", Qualification ensures balance and stability by evaluating outcomes and validating the project's alignment with its objectives.
   a. Evaluating Outcomes: Evaluating the overall outcome of each module as a group of functionalities to find enhancement points.
   b. Validating project: Validating the project's alignment (Project as HIS Implementation or mini-projects (Task Forces) as HIS Sub-Systems Implementation with its objectives.

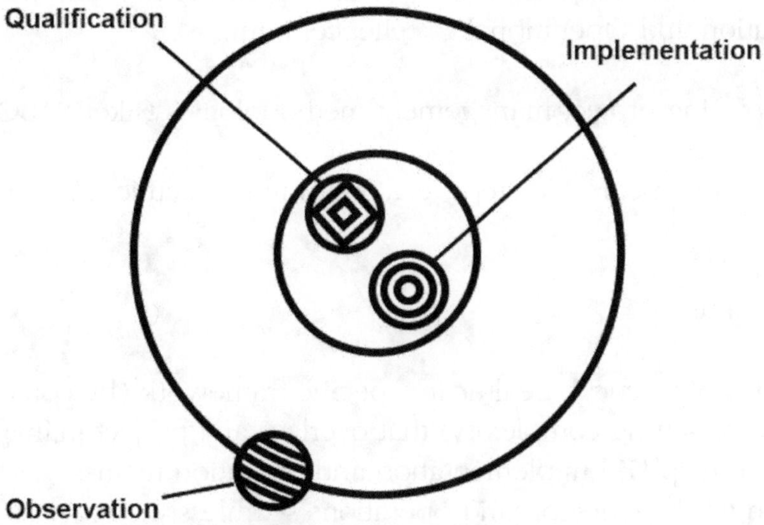

Figure 2.1 Core interaction model: conceptual model

The interplay of these elements creates a cohesive system where each particle's role is interdependent, contributing to the overall stability and functionality of the project (Figure 2.1 and Figure 2.2).

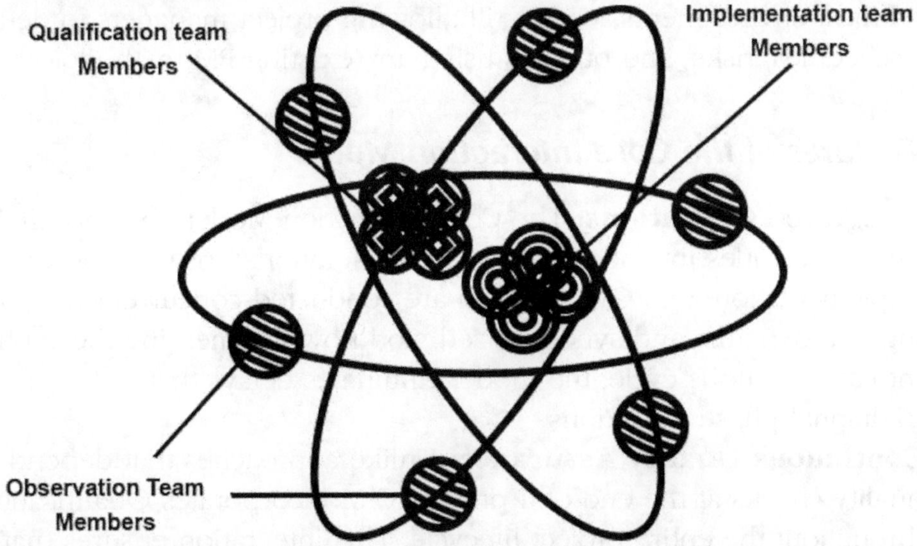

Figure 2.2 Core interaction model: conceptual model

With the Core Interaction Model (CIM): A Continuous Framework for HIS Implementation and Operational Excellence, I am:

- Not replacing project management methodologies (like PMBOK, Agile, PRINCE2, etc.).
- Not redefining core PM steps (e.g., planning, execution, monitoring, and closing).

But rather, I am:

- Providing a practical, healthcare-specific framework (by considering the healthcare setting complexity) that overlays any project management model to help HIS implementation and operation teams:
  - Align implementation and operations seamlessly.
  - Maintain continuous stakeholder interaction.
  - Embed performance, feedback, and adaptation in real time.
  - Avoid phase fragmentation and role confusion that often occur in hospital environments.

Think of CIM as a strategic interaction and performance layer that guides how the people, processes, and systems should behave and evolve in complex, clinical environments, while still allowing project managers to define tasks, schedules, risks, and budgets using any existing PM methodology.

Key Features of the Core Interaction Model

1. **Integrated Operations:** The Core Interaction Model does not divide project activities into separate phases or iterations. Instead, Observation, Implementation, and Qualification are conducted concurrently, resulting in a dynamic and synchronized workflow. By merging these phases into a continuous cycle, the model eliminates delays that may arise from traditional phase transitions.
2. **Continuous Quality Assurance:** Unlike approaches that depend on quality checks at the end of a project, CIM incorporates Qualification throughout the entire project lifecycle. This integration ensures that quality is embedded in every activity and phase. Deliverables are evaluated regularly and iteratively to confirm that they meet operational, clinical, and strategic objectives, while consistently maintaining high standards.

3. **Dynamic Feedback Loops:** Ongoing interaction among project elements establishes real-time feedback loops. This structure allows for the prompt identification of issues and the immediate implementation of corrective measures.
4. **Holistic Alignment:** The model is designed to ensure that all components remain aligned with stakeholder objectives. This alignment minimizes miscommunication and reduces the risk of misalignment throughout the project lifecycle.
5. **Observation-Driven Analysis:** CIM emphasizes structured and continuous analysis during project execution. This approach captures operational insights from real-world scenarios and enables dynamic refinement of system requirements.
6. **Agility and Incremental Development:** Drawing on iterative methodologies, CIM supports rapid feedback and incremental improvements. This flexibility allows the system to adapt quickly to changing requirements and evolving project needs.
7. **Collaborative and Cross-Functional Teams:** The model ensures active involvement from all stakeholders, including implementation teams, operational staff, and end users. This collaborative approach facilitates the co-creation of effective solutions.
8. **Performance as a Core Metric:** CIM places a strong emphasis on performance improvement, focusing on system usability, operational effectiveness, and stakeholder satisfaction as key measures of success.
9. **Adaptable to Complexity:** The model is specifically designed to manage the complexities of large-scale projects, such as Health Information System (HIS) implementations. It maintains flexibility while preserving a clear and organized structure.

Benefits for Core Interaction Model in HIS Implementations

Applying the Core Interaction Model to HIS projects offers several unique advantages:

- **Enhanced Stakeholder Engagement:** Ongoing observation facilitates clear communication and alignment with all stakeholders throughout the project lifecycle.
- **Stakeholder Satisfaction:** Consistent engagement and rapid feedback cycles ensure that the needs of end users and stakeholders are addressed promptly and effectively.

- **Real-Time Adaptability:** The model's dynamic structure allows the project team to respond efficiently to changes in scope and unforeseen challenges as they arise.
- **Embedded Quality Control:** Integrated qualification processes help reduce the likelihood of rework and ensure that deliverables comply with both organizational and regulatory requirements.
- **Unified Approach:** By integrating observation, implementation, and qualification into a single, cohesive system, the model promotes stability and consistency in project execution.
- **Reduced Downtime and Risk:** The combination of implementation and operational activities minimizes disruptions and supports steady project progress.
- **Seamless Transition Between Phases:** This approach removes the need for a distinct end to the implementation phase, enabling a smooth and continuous development process.
- **Performance-Centric Approach:** Each cycle delivers measurable improvements in usability, efficiency, and overall system performance.

What Makes Core Interaction Model to Work

This model eliminates the need for multiple iterative development cycles of varying sizes to collect user feedback on different software features within a Hospital Information System (HIS). Instead, feedback is gathered continuously throughout both the development and implementation phases. This approach allows for greater flexibility in refining software features and enables rapid implementation.

By not allocating time to the creation of separate software cycles, the process of development, observation, feedback collection, and subsequent improvement of software features proceeds at a significantly accelerated pace.

Hybrid project management approaches combine elements of predictive and adaptive methods to address uncertainty while maintaining control[13]. However, successful adoption of these models requires the implementation team to have a strong understanding of various project management methodologies. This expertise is necessary to effectively combine different approaches.

Despite these advantages, there is an increased risk to overall efficiency in environments such as HIS implementation. In these settings, end users play a vital role in enhancing and utilizing system features, yet they often lack specialized knowledge of project management. This gap is a significant factor contributing to higher costs and extended timelines commonly observed in Hospital Information System (HIS) implementation projects.

The Core Interaction Model assigns stakeholders to roles that align with their expertise. This approach enables each group to apply its specific skills to improve the quality of Health Information System (HIS) implementation, enhance flexibility, and minimize both costs and implementation time.

Development Team: Responsible for all aspects of system development.

Observation Team: Handles planning and monitoring activities throughout the process.

Quality Team: Ensures overall quality and maintains a balance between observation and implementation efforts.

How CIM Addresses HIS Implementation and Operation Challenges

Berg describes HIS/PCIS implementation as a process of mutual transformation between organization and technology and stresses organizational transformation and management/user support[8].

Several strategies are available for implementing the Hospital Information System (HIS), including the "big-bang", "parallel", and "step-by-step" approaches. In addition, various project and operation management frameworks, such as the Microsoft Operation Framework (MOF), may be employed. The chosen strategy and management model significantly influence planning, resource allocation, budgeting, delivery timelines, and the overall quality of operations.

Each implementation strategy presents distinct levels of risk, resource requirements, and impact on users. The appropriate choice depends on the specific needs, available resources, and complexity of the organization. As a result, hospitals and healthcare centers may adopt different approaches based on their unique circumstances.

A primary challenge in this process arises when the implementation strategy selected by the hospital does not align with the project management methodology used by the technical team. Such discrepancies can have a significant effect on the success of the project.

The Core Interaction Model (CIM) addresses this challenge by ensuring that all stakeholders are engaged in coordinated and synchronized cycles, regardless of the chosen strategy or management framework. CIM is a stakeholder-centered approach to the implementation and operation of the Hospital Information System (HIS). It functions through continuous cycles of planning, feedback, and execution, involving key participants from clinical, administrative, technical, managerial, and legal domains (Table 2.1).

The Core Interaction Model (CIM) fundamentally changes the way Hospital Information Systems (HIS) are implemented and operated. By fostering collaboration among stakeholders, CIM enhances system usability, affordability, and sustainability.

The Project Management Institute (PMI) has defined key knowledge areas essential for effective project management. Within each project, dedicated working groups are assigned responsibilities aligned with these scientific domains. The following table outlines how the Core Interaction Model (CIM) supports and aligns with each Project Management Knowledge Area and its associated Process Groups (Table 2.2).

Implementing a Hospital Information System (HIS) is a multifaceted undertaking that requires careful planning and organization. The Project Management Institute's Project Management Body of Knowledge (PMBOK)

Table 2.1 Key Benefits of a Collaborative and Structured HIS Implementation and Operation Approach through Core Interaction Model (CIM)

Benefits	Description
Reduces implementation costs	Improves planning, avoids unnecessary customizations, and enables phased rollouts.
Minimizes resistance to change	Actively engages end-users from the start, fostering inclusion, trust, and tailored training.
Boosts sharing responsibility	Encourages shared responsibility, real-time collaboration, and continuous awareness.
Adapts to clinical workflows	Incorporates real-time feedback and user-driven adjustments instead of rigid assumptions.
Ensures regulatory compliance	Involves Quality and compliance teams early and continuously.
Addresses skill gaps	Promotes knowledge-sharing and internal capacity building during implementation and Operation.
Supports ongoing maintenance	Enables integrated observation, evaluation, and upgrade planning.
Strengthens stakeholder engagement	Maintains constant communication and alignment, preventing miscommunication and priority conflicts.

Table 2.2 How CIM Supports Corresponding Project Process Group in Different Project Management Area

Project Management Area	Corresponding Project Process Group	How CIM Supports It
Project Integration Management	Project Start: Create the project charter	CIM ensures early involvement of all stakeholders, aligning project vision and creating a realistic, co-created charter.
Project Scope Management	Planning: Develop the project management plan	CIM enables a clear understanding of scope through continuous dialogue, reducing scope creep and ensuring stakeholder alignment.
Project Schedule Management	Execution: Execute the project management plan	CIM's iterative cycles ensure flexibility in execution and allow real-time adaptation of the schedule to match evolving realities.
Project Cost Management	Monitoring and Control: Control activities and costs Planning: Estimate costs, plan resource acquisition, and define budget	CIM reduces rework and unnecessary features, ensuring smarter budgeting and spending based on continuous feedback. It also allows phased implementation to manage costs better.
Project Closure Management	Closing: Project closure	Through its iterative cycles, CIM ensures alignment and continuous documentation, facilitating a smoother closure process and lessons learned capture.
Project Objectives and Vision Management	Across all groups	CIM engages all stakeholders from the start to co-define objectives and maintains ongoing alignment through feedback cycles, helping prevent deviation from goals.
Project Time Management	Planning: Define, sequence, and estimate activities Monitoring: Control the schedule	CIM's collaborative planning supports accurate time estimation. Regular feedback allows timely adjustments to prevent delays.

(*Continued*)

Table 2.2 (Continued) How CIM Supports Corresponding Project Process Group in Different Project Management Area

Project Management Area	Corresponding Project Process Group	How CIM Supports It
Project Quality Management	Planning: Plan for quality Execution: Ensure quality Monitoring: Control quality	By involving real users in feedback loops, CIM ensures quality standards are defined clearly, met practically, and evaluated continuously.
Project Human Resource Management	Planning: HR and organizational planning Execution: Team formation and management Closing: Release resources	CIM supports distributed responsibility, team learning, and cross-functional engagement. Team performance is sustained through collaboration.
Project Communication Management	All groups	CIM is communication-centric: It identifies stakeholders, creates shared understanding, ensures constant information flow, and aligns expectations throughout the project lifecycle.
Project Risk Management	Planning: Identify, assess, and respond to risks Monitoring: Monitor and control risks	CIM enables early risk identification through stakeholder insights and supports agile responses through its continuous feedback and iteration model.
Project Procurement Management	Planning: Develop plan and requests Execution: Issue and manage contracts Monitoring and Control: Monitor contracts Closing: Close contracts	By keeping vendors involved in collaborative cycles, CIM enhances requirement clarity, manages expectations, and improves contract outcomes.

provides a structured framework that can guide this process effectively. The following outlines the practical phases recommended by PMI, aligned with the Clinical Information Management (CIM) model, and highlights the key stages to address within each phase.

PMI Phase 1: Initiation

- Objective: Define the project's vision, objectives, feasibility, and stakeholder identification.

How CIM Covers This Phase

- Observation (Identifying Needs):
  - Captures project objectives (patient safety, care quality, operational efficiency, cost reduction, etc.) clearly from hospital informatics and clinical experts.
  - Engages stakeholders continuously, ensuring alignment from the project's outset.
- Qualification (Validating Project):
  - Ensures initial project objectives align with the broader strategic, operational, and clinical goals.
  - Performs initial validation of project feasibility through continuous analysis rather than a single-stage review.

Key PMI Areas Covered

- Project Charter Development
- Stakeholder Identification and Engagement
- Feasibility Study

PMI Phase 2: Planning

- Objective: Establish project roadmap, define detailed scope, risk management, resources, cost, schedule, quality standards, procurement, and communication strategies.

How CIM Covers This Phase

- Observation (Identifying Needs):
  - Requirements gathering and analysis performed dynamically, allowing continuous adaptation.
- Implementation (Technical Analysis, Functional Design & Configuration):
  - Detailed system architecture planning occurs early, supporting dynamic and incremental planning processes.
  - Functional design (electronic forms, reports, and workflows) is defined interactively with end users and technical teams.
- Qualification (Evaluating Outcomes):
  - Early definition and continuous verification of quality management plans, risk mitigation strategies, and continuous quality assurance standards.

Key PMI Areas Covered

- Requirements Gathering
- Scope Definition and Work Breakdown Structure (WBS)
- Risk Management Plan
- Time and Cost Estimation
- Communications Plan
- Quality Management Plan
- Procurement Planning

PMI Phase 3: Execution

- Objective: Implement the HIS according to the project plan through configuration, integration, data migration, user training, change management, stakeholder engagement, and cultural transformation.

How CIM Covers This Phase

- Implementation (Development, Technical Analysis, and Technical Testing):
  - Ongoing development based on stakeholder and end-user feedback ensures alignment of configuration and integration activities.

  - Technical testing integrated continuously rather than as a final step, allowing rapid corrective actions.
- Observation (Monitoring Progress, Gathering Insights):
  - Real-time monitoring of system configuration, data migration, and integration activities.
  - Continuous collection of user insights enhances user training effectiveness and aligns with hospital workflows.
- Qualification (Evaluating Outcomes):
  - Continuously evaluates execution outcomes to quickly identify necessary adjustments, thereby supporting effective change management.
  - Supports culture transformation by embedding quality and continuous improvement throughout implementation.

Key PMI Areas Covered

- System Configuration
- Data Migration
- Integration with Other Systems
- User Training
- Change Management
- Stakeholder Management and Communication
- Cultural Transformation

PMI Phase 4: Monitoring and Controlling

- Objective: Track progress, manage scope, monitor risks, resolve issues, and ensure continuous quality during implementation.

How CIM Covers This Phase

- Observation (Monitoring Progress, Gathering Insights):
  - Continuous real-time tracking of project progress against KPIs.
  - Immediate identification and management of project risks and scope variations.
- Qualification (Evaluating Outcomes, Validating Project):
  - Constant monitoring and validation against quality standards, operational performance criteria, and user satisfaction.
  - Continuous evaluation and iterative adjustment based on real-time feedback.

- Implementation (Technical Testing and Development):
  - Rapid iterative adjustments and ongoing refinement of the system based on control measures and feedback loops.

Key PMI Areas Covered

- Performance Monitoring (KPIs)
- Issue Management
- Scope Control
- Quality Control and Testing
- Risk Monitoring

PMI Phase 5: Closing

- Objective: Finalize HIS implementation, validate system readiness, deploy the system, conduct post-implementation review, ensure documentation handover, and provide support after go-live.

How CIM Covers This Phase

- Qualification (Evaluating Outcomes, Validating Project):
  - Continuous validation facilitates a smooth transition to operational use with minimal surprises during go-live.
  - Ensures comprehensive and continuous documentation of lessons learned throughout, streamlining the final documentation handover.
- Implementation (System Go-Live):
  - Seamless transition from implementation to operation, supporting continuous enhancements post-go-live.
- Observation (Gathering Insights):
  - Continues to gather feedback immediately post-launch to swiftly address user concerns, enhancing early post-implementation support.

Key PMI Areas Covered

- Final Testing and Validation
- System Go-Live and Deployment
- Post-Implementation Review
- Documentation Handover
- Project Closure Report
- Post-Go-Live Support

So in summary, how does CIM enhance PMI's structure?

- Integrated Continuous Flow: CIM merges initiation, planning, execution, and monitoring into a continuous, interactive cycle, providing real-time responsiveness and adaptability.
- Real-Time Agility: CIM emphasizes continuous observation and rapid integration of feedback, significantly reducing response times and improving project adaptability.
- Embedded Quality Assurance: Quality validation is not confined to one phase but embedded throughout CIM, reducing rework, enhancing project efficiency, and ensuring the final product aligns closely with stakeholder expectations.
- Deep Stakeholder Integration: CIM deeply integrates stakeholder engagement at every stage, surpassing typical PMI stakeholder engagement expectations, which are often limited to specific project phases.
- Reduced Risks and Costs: CIM's continuous iterative approach effectively addresses risk management and cost control by enabling early issue detection and resolution.

Core Principles for HIS Implementation and Operation Management (Reflecting the Principles of CIM)

Current findings suggest that EHR/HIS implementation projects produce effects across clinical work, patient care, and economic impact, broader than "just Information Technology"[14]. Supported by socio-technical framing: successful implementation depends on understanding interrelated social, technical, and environmental factors and is "challenging", with failure risk discussed in the literature[15]. Success depends on adopting an approach that extends beyond traditional project management and operational frameworks. It is essential to address the transformation of clinical workflows, administrative procedures, and user behaviors. Meaningful use of EHR/HIS depends on successful integration into clinical workflow and that adopting HIT requires behavior change and process mapping/adaptation[16].

The risk of failure in such projects is considerable. Many initiatives exceed their budgets, miss critical deadlines, or fail to deliver functional solutions. Frequently, these outcomes result from neglecting fundamental project management principles (Table 2.3).

Table 2.3 Summary: Alignment of CIM with PMI Phases

PMI Phases	Observation	Implementation	Qualification
Initiation	Needs Identification and Stakeholder Engagement	Resource/Technical Feasibility	Project Alignment and Validation
Planning	Requirements Gathering, Design and Scope Definition	System Architecture and Module Design	Risk Assessment, Quality Standards
Execution	Continuous User Feedback and Monitoring	Continuous Development and Integration	Iterative Quality and Change Management
Monitoring and Controlling	Real-Time Progress Monitoring	Rapid Adjustments and Technical Refinements	Continuous Outcome Evaluation and Quality Assurance
Closing	Post-Go-Live Insights and User Acceptance	Smooth Go-Live and Ongoing Enhancements	Continuous Validation and Final Documentation

A structured methodology that accounts for the unique challenges of healthcare environments, the interests of diverse stakeholders, and the need for ongoing adaptation is crucial. Without such an approach, even the most advanced technical systems may not achieve their intended objectives. The principles outlined above, based on the Core Interaction Model, are designed to address these challenges effectively throughout both implementation and operational phases.

The following principles are based on the foundational elements of the CIM framework. They highlight the importance of real-time feedback, cross-functional collaboration, and system usability. Supported by evidence calling for rapid-cycle, continuous feedback from users to guide design/implementation and highlighting usability/STS considerations[17]. By adhering to these principles, Hospital Information System (HIS) projects are positioned to fulfill technical requirements while also providing tangible benefits to patients, clinicians, and hospital leadership.

Continuous Stakeholder Engagement

- Why it matters: HIS projects span departments, roles, and hierarchies in clinical, administrative, and technical areas. Active, ongoing involvement ensures alignment and builds ownership.
- CIM Link: Embedded in observation through real-time feedback, need identification, and continuous communication.
- Implementation Tip: Build a structured framework for stakeholder communication, such as regular feedback cycles, joint workshops, and embedded liaisons (example medical informatics experts).

Real-Time Observation and Feedback Integration

- Why it matters: Unlike traditional systems, HIS is mission-critical and evolves with user needs and legal regulations. Static analysis is not enough.
- CIM Link: Central to observation; enables dynamic adaptation and immediate insight gathering.
- Implementation Tip: Use embedded observers (project champions, floor super-users) to provide live operational feedback during the implementation.

Simultaneous Execution and Quality Assurance

- Why it matters: Waiting until the end to validate outcomes leads to costly rework in healthcare settings.
- CIM Link: Seamless interaction between Implementation and Qualification, ensuring testing and refinement occur continuously.
- Implementation Tip: Implement rolling validations and pilot testing with real users as features are released.

Incremental and Adaptive Delivery

- Why it matters: HIS implementations cannot afford long release cycles. Adaptive rollouts reduce risk and allow fast course correction.
- CIM Link: Observed through the Agility and Incremental Development characteristics of CIM.

- Implementation Tip: Structure delivery as a series of manageable enhancements (micro-releases), with operational value and user feedback loops.

Performance-Centric Progress Measurement

- Why it matters: Measuring success in HIS must go beyond timelines and budgets. System usability, clinical effectiveness, and operational efficiency matter more.
- CIM Link: Performance is a core metric in CIM, especially emphasized in Qualification.
- Implementation Tip: Define KPIs that measure both system performance (example response time) and user outcomes (example patient throughput, clinician satisfaction).

Integrated Operations and Implementation

- Why it matters: HIS systems are not isolated software projects. They're embedded in day-to-day hospital operations.
- CIM Link: This principle is the foundation of CIM: No strict separation between “project” and “operation”.
- Implementation Tip: Blend go-live preparations with real operations through shadowing, phased activations, and joint support desks.

Domain-Centered Role Assignment

- Why it matters: Not everyone needs to be a project manager, but everyone needs to know their exact role and how it impacts HIS success.
- CIM Link: CIM clearly differentiates Observation, Implementation, and Qualification roles across stakeholders.
- Implementation Tip: Assign responsibilities clearly: Let developers develop, IT staff observe and configure, and quality teams validate usability and integration.

Cultural Transformation as a Strategic Objective

- Why it matters: Technology adoption in healthcare is heavily influenced by culture and mindset.

- CIM Link: Implicitly supported by continuous stakeholder engagement, feedback loops, and collaboration.
- Implementation Tip: Include behavior change strategies in the project plan, celebrate quick wins, train change champions, and communicate benefits constantly.

Resilience and Responsiveness to Change

- Why it matters: Healthcare regulations, technologies, and hospital priorities change fast. Your project must pivot smoothly.
- CIM Link: Enabled by dynamic feedback loops and Observation-Driven Analysis.
- Implementation Tip: Create buffer capacity in your plan for change requests, and document a rapid decision-making protocol.

Unified, Cross-Functional Team Collaboration

- Why it matters: HIS is at the intersection of IT, clinical care, finance, and management; no single department can implement it alone.
- CIM Link: Fully embedded through Collaborative and Cross-Functional Teams.
- Implementation Tip: Design multidisciplinary task forces that persist throughout the implementation and post-live stabilization.

Rapid Learning and Evolution

- Why it matters: Hospitals are learning environments; your HIS must be too.
- CIM Link: Reinforced by continuous qualification and iterative cycles of development and validation.
- Implementation Tip: Run retrospectives and rapid reviews after each major release or workflow change.

System Usability and User Empowerment

- Why it matters: If clinicians can't or won't use the system, the project fails, regardless of budget or technical performance.
- CIM Link: Performance in CIM includes usability and stakeholder satisfaction as core goals.

- Implementation Tip: Design for intuitive use, conduct live demos, and provide role-based training tailored to end-user needs.

In the next chapter, we will explore each of these principles and more in detail, breaking down how they apply in real-world HIS implementation and operation scenarios and offering practical guidance on how to apply them effectively. By understanding and adopting these principles, project and operation teams can significantly reduce risk, improve collaboration, and deliver systems that truly enhance healthcare delivery. Whether you're part of a hospital leadership team, an IT specialist, or a vendor partner, these insights will help you navigate the complexities of HIS projects with greater clarity and confidence.

NOTE:

CIM is a practical framework based on experience. It does not replace formal project governance. It should be adapted to organizational context.

References

1. Hundal GS, Rhodes D, Laux C. Digital transformation of healthcare enterprises in the era of disruptions—a structured literature review. *Sustainability.* 2025;17(13):5690. https://doi.org/10.3390/su17135690
2. Menachemi N, Collum TH. Benefits and drawbacks of electronic health record systems. *Risk Manag Healthc Policy.* 2011;4:47–55. doi:10.2147/RMHP.S12985.
3. Cresswell K, Sheikh A. Organizational issues in the implementation and adoption of health information technology innovations: An interpretative review. *Int J Med Inform.* 2013;82(5):e73–e86. doi:10.1016/j.ijmedinf.2012.10.007
4. Tun SYY, Madanian S. Critical success factors in clinical information system implementation: A systematic review. *J Am Med Inform Assoc.* 2023;30(3):546–556.
5. Greenhalgh T, Robert G, Macfarlane F, Bate P, Kyriakidou O. Diffusion of innovations in service organizations: Systematic review and recommendations. *Milbank Q.* 2004;82(4):581–629. doi:10.1111/j.0887-378X.2004.00325.x
6. Heeks R. Health information systems: Failure, success, and improvisation. *Inf Syst J.* 2006;16(3):279–295.
7. Laudon KC, Laudon JP. *Management Information Systems.* 15th ed. Pearson; 2018.

8. Berg M. Implementing information systems in healthcare organizations: Myths and challenges. *Int J Med Inform.* 2001;64(2–3):143–156. doi:10.1016/s1386-5056(01)00200-3
9. Sittig DF, Singh H. Sociotechnical approach to EHR safety. *J Am Med Inform Assoc.* 2010;17(4):377–382.
10. Sommerville I. *Software Engineering.* 10th ed. Pearson; 2016.
11. Ash JS, et al. Stakeholder participation in health IT. *J Am Med Inform Assoc.* 2007;14(4):542–549.
12. Pollack J, Adler D. Emergent trends in project management. *Int J Proj Manag.* 2016;34(2):226–238.
13. Pollack J, Adler D. Emergent trends and challenges in project management. *Int J Proj Manag.* 2016;34(2):226–238.
14. Tsai CH, Eghdam A, Davoody N, Wright G, Flowerday S, Koch S. Effects of electronic health record implementation and barriers to adoption and use: A scoping review and qualitative analysis of the content. *Life (Basel).* 2020;10(12):327. Published December 4, 2020. doi:10.3390/life10120327
15. Irizarry T, Barton AJ. A sociotechnical approach to successful electronic health record implementation: Five best practices for clinical nurse specialists. *Clin Nurse Spec.* 2013;27(6):283–285. doi:10.1097/NUR.0b013e3182a872e3
16. Yusif S, Hafeez-Baig A, Soar J. Change management and adoption of health information technology (HIT)/eHealth in public hospitals in Ghana: A qualitative study. *Appl Comput Inform.* 2022;18(3–4):279–289. doi:10.1016/j.aci.2019.11.007.
17. Wesley DB, Schubel L, Hsiao CJ, et al. A socio-technical systems approach to the use of health IT for patient reported outcomes: Patient and healthcare provider perspectives. *J Biomed Inform.* 2019;100(Suppl):100048. doi:10.1016/j.yjbinx.2019.100048.

Chapter 3

Translating Strategy into Action: HIS Implementation and Operation Management Principles in Practice

Continuous Stakeholder Engagement

Hospital Information System (HIS) projects encompass a wide range of departments, roles, and hierarchical levels, including clinical, administrative, and technical areas. Literature describing EHR/HIS implementation as an enterprise-wide transformation affecting multidisciplinary stakeholders across clinical, administrative, and IT domains[1]. Consistent and active participation from all involved parties is essential to maintain alignment and foster a sense of ownership throughout the project lifecycle.

Effective implementation of HIS requires real-time feedback and ongoing communication among all identified stakeholders. Socio-technical systems literature emphasizing continuous feedback loops, communication, and participatory implementation strategies[2]. The process of stakeholder identification is critical and entails recognizing every individual and group affected by, or capable of influencing, the project. Project management and health IT implementation research identifying stakeholder identification as foundational for project success[3]. This includes clinical staff, administrators, IT teams, and external vendors.

Gaining a clear understanding of each stakeholder's roles, requirements, and concerns at an early stage supports alignment, minimizes resistance, and promotes meaningful engagement as the project progresses. Change

 DOI: 10.4324/9781003795254-3

management literature in healthcare IT emphasizing early stakeholder analysis to reduce resistance and improve alignment[4].

Here are some practical tips for Identifying stakeholders:

- Stakeholder Interviews: Conduct one-on-one interviews with key personnel, such as department heads, clinical staff, and IT teams, to gather insights on who should be involved or impacted by the HIS implementation. This ensures a deeper understanding of individual and department-specific needs.
- Surveys and Questionnaires: Distribute surveys to a wide range of hospital staff to collect information on potential stakeholders who interact with current systems. This method helps reach a broader audience and uncover stakeholders who might not be immediately obvious.
- Organizational Process Mapping: Map out the hospital's workflows and processes to identify all departments and roles that interact with patient information or Hospital Information System (HIS). This visual approach helps highlight all areas affected by the HIS implementation, revealing relevant stakeholders.
- Consultation with Senior Leadership: Engage senior management and hospital leadership to provide insights into high-level stakeholders, external partners, or regulatory bodies that might not be immediately apparent but are critical to the project's success, ensuring no key influencers are missed.
- Conduct a Stakeholder Mapping Session: Gather a diverse group of project team members to brainstorm all potential stakeholders, including internal (example doctors, nurses, and IT staff) and external (example vendors, regulatory bodies) parties, to ensure no one is overlooked.
- Involve Department Heads Early: Engage leaders from key departments (example clinical, administrative, IT) at the beginning of the project to help identify both obvious and less obvious stakeholders, especially frontline staff who will use the system regularly.
- Use a RACI Matrix: Create a RACI (Responsible, Accountable, Consulted, and Informed) matrix to clearly define the roles of each stakeholder, ensuring that everyone's involvement and influence on the project are properly identified and documented.

Although identifying stakeholders is widely recognized as a critical factor in achieving project success, many projects continue to encounter difficulties in this area. These challenges do not typically arise from a lack of understanding regarding their significance. Rather, they often stem from recurring mistakes and apprehensions.

Below are some of the common issues that contribute to these challenges:

- Mistake: Overlooking Key Stakeholders:
  - Fear: The HIS manager might fear involving too many stakeholders will complicate decision-making, leading to overlooking critical individuals or groups, such as end-users or external partners, who could significantly impact the project.
- Mistake: Assuming Stakeholder Roles are Static:
  - Fear: The HIS manager might mistakenly assume that stakeholder roles won't change over time, failing to recognize that new stakeholders may emerge, or existing stakeholders may shift roles as the project progresses, which can lead to gaps in communication or missed input.
- Mistake: Focusing Only on High-Level Stakeholders:
  - Fear: The manager may fear that involving frontline staff or lower-level employees early in the process will slow things down. This could result in only engaging executives or department heads, which can lead to a system that doesn't address the practical needs of the actual users.

Accurately identifying stakeholders is an essential initial step in the implementation and operation of the Hospital Information System (HIS). However, without clear communication among stakeholders, meaningful engagement cannot be achieved. The following activities are recommended to enhance the effectiveness of stakeholder communication:

- Create a Stakeholder Communication Plan:
  Develop a detailed communication plan that outlines how, when, and through which channels (example meetings, emails, and reports) updates and information will be shared with different stakeholder groups. This ensures consistency and prevents miscommunication.
- Hold Regular Cross-Functional Meetings:
  Schedule regular meetings with representatives from various departments (clinical, administrative, and IT) to provide updates, gather feedback, and address concerns. These meetings help keep everyone aligned and engaged.

- Use Visual Dashboards:
  Implement project management tools or dashboards that visually display project progress, milestones, and timelines. This gives stakeholders a clear, real-time overview of the implementation's status without needing detailed technical explanations.
- Tailor Communication to the Audience:
  Customize the level of detail and technical language based on the stakeholder group. For example, use simple, high-level summaries for executives, while providing more detailed technical information for IT teams. This ensures the message resonates with its audience.

Fears and Mistakes in stakeholder communication:

- Mistake: Assuming Everyone is on the Same Page:
  - Fear: The HIS manager might fear that excessive communication could overwhelm stakeholders, leading them to under-communicate. This can result in misalignment, where different teams have varying understandings of project goals, timelines, and expectations.
- Mistake: Not Addressing Stakeholder-Specific Concerns:
  - Fear: The HIS manager might hesitate to customize messages for different stakeholders, worrying it will take too much time or cause inconsistencies. This can lead to some stakeholders feeling left out or uninformed.
- Mistake: Delaying Bad News:
  - Fear: The manager might fear delivering bad news, such as delays or issues, to stakeholders, hoping to resolve the problem first. This can lead to a loss of trust if stakeholders feel problems are being hidden from them.

Training and support are essential components in engaging stakeholders during the implementation of a Hospital Information System (HIS). Empirical studies demonstrate that training and user support are core determinants of successful EHR adoption[5]. These elements help to build confidence, minimize resistance, and enable users to participate actively in the process. When stakeholders receive adequate training and support, they are more inclined to adopt the system, offer constructive feedback, and contribute to its overall success. Technology acceptance and healthcare IT adoption research demonstrating training improves adoption and system utilization[6].

Effective training programs and accessible support channels ensure that users gain a clear understanding of both the operational aspects and the underlying purpose of the new system. This comprehensive approach fosters stronger commitment among users and facilitates a smoother transition throughout the implementation phase.

The following activities are recommended to enhance the effectiveness of training and support initiatives:

- Hands-On Workshops:
  Conduct interactive, role-specific workshops that allow stakeholders to use the HIS in real-world scenarios. This builds confidence and familiarity with the system, encouraging active participation and feedback during the implementation process.
- Super-User Training Program:
  Identify and train "super-users" within different departments who can act as local experts. They provide ongoing support and act as liaisons between the implementation team and their peers, ensuring continuous engagement and troubleshooting.
- Customized Training Materials:
  Develop training materials tailored to the specific needs of each stakeholder group, such as video tutorials, user manuals, and cheat sheets, ensuring that users at all levels receive the appropriate level of guidance.
- Post-Launch Support Desk:
  Set up a dedicated support desk or hotline that stakeholders can access after the system goes live. This ensures that any issues or concerns are addressed promptly, reinforcing stakeholder trust and confidence in the system.

Fears and Mistakes in Stakeholder Training and Support:

- Mistake: Inadequate Training:
  - Fear: The manager might fear that extensive training will take too much time and resources, leading to rushed or insufficient training sessions. This can cause users to feel unprepared and frustrated when using the system.
- Mistake: Overlooking Role-Specific Needs:
  - Fear: The manager might worry about creating too many different training programs, leading to a one-size-fits-all approach. This can

result in training that doesn't meet the specific needs of different user groups, decreasing overall effectiveness.

- Mistake: Neglecting Post-Implementation Support:
  - Fear: The manager might assume that once the system is live, users will be able to manage on their own. This neglect of ongoing support can lead to unresolved issues, user frustration, and poor system adoption.

Change management is essential in facilitating stakeholder engagement, particularly during the implementation of Hospital Information System (HIS). It assists individuals and teams in managing the transition process by addressing concerns, minimizing resistance, and fostering trust. This is achieved through early involvement of stakeholders, clear communication, and providing the necessary support to help them adapt to new systems.

When change is managed effectively, stakeholders are more likely to feel acknowledged, respected, and empowered. This approach encourages stronger collaboration and enables a smoother adoption of the system.

Key Activities to Enhance Change Management Effectiveness:

- Early Involvement and Participation:
  Involve key stakeholders from the start to ensure they have a sense of ownership in the project. This could include workshops or focus groups where they contribute to system design, ensuring their needs are considered.
- Change Champions or Ambassadors:
  Identify influential staff members within departments to act as "change champions". These individuals can help communicate the benefits of the HIS, address concerns, and foster a positive attitude toward the change among their peers.
- Transparent and Continuous Communication:
  Maintain an open line of communication with all stakeholders, updating them on the project's progress, potential challenges, and how those are being addressed. Regular newsletters, meetings, or a project portal can help keep everyone informed and aligned.
- Tailored Training and Support Plans:
  Develop role-specific training and support that focuses on the particular needs of different stakeholder groups. This ensures that everyone is prepared for the transition, reducing anxiety and resistance by boosting confidence in their ability to use the new system effectively.

Fears and Mistakes in Change Management:

- Mistake: Underestimating Resistance to Change:
  - Fear: The manager might fear confronting resistance and therefore underestimate the level of resistance among staff. This can lead to a lack of proactive change management strategies, causing delays and pushback during implementation.
- Mistake: Failing to Involve Key Stakeholders Early:
  - Fear: The manager might worry that involving too many people early on will slow down decision-making. However, failing to involve key stakeholders can lead to a lack of buy-in and significant resistance later in the project.
- Mistake: Neglecting the Emotional Impact of Change:
  - Fear: The manager might focus solely on the technical aspects of the change, fearing that addressing emotional or psychological impacts is not their responsibility. This oversight can lead to significant resistance and disengagement from staff who feel anxious or uncertain about the new system.

How Observation in CIM Strengthens Stakeholder Engagement

The Core Interaction Model (CIM) is instrumental in facilitating stakeholder engagement, particularly through its Observation component. Observation is not a passive process; rather, it is a systematic and ongoing approach that involves identifying needs, monitoring progress, and gathering real-time feedback from users in all hospital departments.

By incorporating observers, such as medical informatics specialists, super-users, or IT liaisons, CIM maintains consistent, two-way communication throughout both implementation and operational phases. This structure allows the project team to identify issues promptly, respond to stakeholder concerns, and adjust training and change management strategies as needed.

Through this continuous process, Observation shifts feedback from a single event to an ongoing, substantive exchange. This approach enhances user participation, fosters trust, and supports the successful adoption of new systems.

Table 3.1 Matrix: Continuous Stakeholder Engagement in HIS Implementation

Component	*Key Activities*	*Practical Tips*	*Fears and Common Mistakes*
1. Stakeholder Identification	- Stakeholder interviews (example dept. heads, clinical, and IT) - Surveys/ questionnaires to wide staff groups - Organizational process mapping - Consult with senior leadership - Stakeholder mapping sessions - Early involvement of dept. heads - RACI matrix for role clarity	- Interview cross-sections of users - Use visuals for process mapping - Document and validate with leadership - Map internal and external stakeholders	- Overlooking key stakeholders due to fear of complexity - Assuming static roles over time - Only focusing on high-level roles while ignoring frontline staff
2. Stakeholder Communication	- Create a communication plan (what/how/when to share) - Hold cross-functional meetings regularly - Use dashboards for visibility - Tailor messages by role	- Send regular updates (newsletters, emails) - Adjust detail level for each group - Hold open forums and town halls	- Assuming shared understanding, leading to misalignment - Avoiding role-specific messaging to save time - Delaying bad news out of fear of backlash
3. Training & Support	- Conduct role-based hands-on workshops - Train department-based "super-users" - Provide tailored materials (videos, cheat sheets) - Set up post-go-live support desk	- Prioritize hands-on practice before go-live - Offer long-term helpdesk support - Use different formats for different learning needs	- Inadequate training due to time/resource fears - Generic, non-role-specific sessions - Assuming support ends post-implementation, leading to user frustration

(*Continued*)

Table 3.1 (Continued) Matrix: Continuous Stakeholder Engagement in HIS Implementation

Component	*Key Activities*	*Practical Tips*	*Fears and Common Mistakes*
4. Change Management	- Early involvement of stakeholders - Identify change champions/ ambassadors - Transparent, ongoing communication - Tailored change training/support	- Assign and empower departmental ambassadors - Provide real-life benefits and outcomes - Address emotional concerns as valid and manageable	- Underestimating resistance and delaying mitigation - Failing to involve stakeholders early, missing buy-in - Ignoring emotional impact, focusing only on technical rollout

Further Reading

- *Managing Stakeholders as Clients: Sponsorship, Partnership, Leadership, and Citizenship*, Mario Henrique Trentim
- *Making Things Happen: Mastering Project Management*, Scott Berkun
- *The Standard for Stakeholder Engagement,* PMI (Project Management Institute)
- *HBR Guide to Managing Up and Across*, Harvard Business Review Press
- *Organizational Change: An Action-Oriented Toolkit*, Tupper Cawsey, and Gene Deszca, Cynthia Ingols
- *Switch: How to Change Things When Change Is Hard*, Chip Heath & Dan Heath
- *The Fifth Discipline: The Art and Practice of the Learning Organization*, Peter Senge
- *User-Centered System Design: New Perspectives on Human-Computer Interaction*, Donald Norman and Stephen Draper
- *PMBOK® Guide*, 7th Edition (PMI): Introduces performance domains like stakeholder, team, and communication management in a more adaptable format.

Real-Time Observation and Feedback Integration

Health IT systems are classified as safety-critical/mission-critical systems that directly impact patient care and must respond to regulatory and workflow changes[7]. Relying solely on static analysis is insufficient for effective implementation.

Feedback mechanisms play a vital role in the successful deployment of HIS. They offer structured channels for users to provide insights, express concerns, and confirm progress in real time. By systematically gathering and addressing stakeholder input, project teams foster trust, ensure the system aligns with operational needs, and promote a sense of shared ownership, all of which are essential for successful adoption. Implementation science literature linking stakeholder engagement to trust-building, workflow alignment, and system acceptance[8].

The following activities and practical tips can significantly enhance the effectiveness of feedback processes:

- Regular Surveys and Polls:

  Use online surveys or quick polls to gather feedback from stakeholders at various stages of the project. Tailor the questions to specific user groups (example doctors, nurses, and IT staff) to ensure relevant feedback is collected and actionable insights are gained.
- Focus Group Discussions:

  Organize small focus group sessions with representatives from different stakeholder groups to discuss their experiences, challenges, and suggestions in detail. This provides deeper insights into concerns and potential areas for improvement.
- User Feedback Portals:

  Set up an easy-to-access online feedback portal where stakeholders can submit suggestions, concerns, or issues at any time. Ensure the portal is monitored, and responses or updates are provided promptly to encourage continuous engagement.
- Feedback loop:

  Implement a process where feedback is not only collected but also acted upon, and users are informed of changes made based on their input.

- Post-Implementation Workshops:
  Conduct workshops after each major milestone or phase of implementation to gather feedback from users about what worked, what didn't, and what could be improved for the next stage. Use these sessions to foster open dialogue and refine the process as needed.

Fears and Mistakes in Feedback Mechanisms:

- Ignoring Negative Feedback:
  - The manager might fear that negative feedback will reflect poorly on the project or their management, leading to a tendency to downplay or ignore it. This can prevent necessary improvements and damage trust with stakeholders.
- Delayed Response to Feedback:
  - The manager might fear that responding to feedback too quickly could lead to hasty decisions, resulting in a slow response process. This can frustrate users and make them feel their input is not valued.
- Failing to Close the Feedback Loop:
  - The manager might assume that collecting feedback is enough and fear that following up with users to inform them of changes made based on their feedback is redundant. However, failing to close the feedback loop can lead to disengagement and a perception that feedback is pointless.

How Observation in CIM Strengthens Feedback Integration

Within the Core Interaction Model (CIM), Observation is established as an ongoing and integrated function throughout the project lifecycle. Rather than being treated as a discrete phase or a task performed at predetermined intervals, Observation remains active at all times. This approach is particularly effective in facilitating the integration of real-time feedback.

Observation in CIM encompasses structured monitoring, active user engagement, and the refinement of requirements. This is achieved through close collaboration with end users, IT personnel, and clinical departments. In contrast to traditional models that depend on periodic reviews, CIM continuously collects, analyzes, and responds to feedback obtained from sources such as surveys, focus groups, and user portals during the entire implementation process.

Table 3.2 Effective Feedback Mechanisms

Component	*Key Activities*	*Practical Tips*	*Fears & Common Mistakes*
1. Structured Feedback Collection	- Regular surveys and polls - Tailored questions by stakeholder type - Focus group discussions - Post-implementation workshops	- Keep surveys short and role-specific - Encourage open discussion in small groups - Schedule feedback right after each project milestone	- Ignoring negative feedback due to fear of criticism - Delaying surveys, missing momentum
2. Continuous Feedback Channels	- Online user feedback portals - Anytime submission of concerns, ideas, and issues	- Ensure 24/7 accessibility - Assign a team to monitor and respond promptly	- Delayed responses due to fear of premature action - Unmonitored portals, causing user frustration
3. Feedback Loop Management	- Establish a formal feedback loop: Collect → act → report back - Communicate what changes were made based on feedback	- Close the loop publicly (example announcements, changelogs) - Highlight improvements as a result of user suggestions	- Failing to close the loop, making users feel unheard - Assuming follow-up is optional, which undermines engagement
4. Post-Implementation Reflection	- Conduct feedback workshops after each phase - Discuss lessons learned, what went well, and improvement points	- Use interactive formats (whiteboards, live polls) - Document lessons and share with all teams	- Fear of opening up sensitive issues - Skipping reflection sessions to save time, losing valuable insights

The model designates specific roles, including medical informatics experts and departmental super-users, to participate in the Observation component. By doing so, CIM maintains a direct and ongoing communication channel between users and the project or operations team. These observers serve as real-time recipients and interpreters of feedback, enabling the early identification of issues, reducing the risk of disengagement, and supporting prompt iteration.

Furthermore, the Observation process in CIM reinforces a continuous feedback-action-feedback cycle. By ensuring that users witness the tangible outcomes of their input, the model fosters trust, encourages greater participation, and expedites the adoption of new systems or processes.

Further Reading

- *The Lean Startup*, Eric Ries
- *Team of Teams*, General Stanley McChrystal
- *Accelerate: The Science of Lean Software and DevOps*, Nicole Forsgren, Jez Humble, and Gene Kim
- *The Fifth Discipline: The Art & Practice of the Learning Organization*, Peter Senge
- *Thinking in Systems: A Primer*, Donella H. Meadows
- *Designing for Behavior Change*, Stephen Wendel
- *Sprint: How to Solve Big Problems and Test New Ideas in Just Five Days*, Jake Knapp et al.
- *User Story Mapping: Discover the Whole Story, Build the Right Product*, Jeff Patton

Simultaneous Execution and Quality Assurance

Delaying outcome validation until the end of a project often results in costly rework within healthcare environments. During this phase, teams are likely to encounter significant challenges. Extended collaboration, particularly under demanding circumstances, can give rise to conflict and heightened tension. Individuals typically respond to these situations in their own ways, and the team may become aware of their differences to some extent. When disagreements occur, team members may react differently; some may appear composed outwardly while managing internal stress. Nevertheless, maintaining self-control contributes to a calmer environment and helps the group navigate periods of tension effectively.

Traditional project management frameworks frequently position quality assurance as a separate phase, usually at the conclusion of the development or implementation process. This practice often leads to the late identification of critical issues, increased rework, and a misalignment between the system and actual operational needs. Software engineering literature comparing waterfall vs iterative models and documenting risks of late defect detection[9]. In the context of Hospital Information System (HIS) projects, where systems have a direct impact on patient care and clinical workflows, it is essential to integrate quality from the outset and sustain it throughout the project life-cycle. Patient safety and health IT safety research emphasizing continuous quality monitoring rather than end-stage validation[7].

The Core Interaction Model (CIM) addresses these challenges by embedding quality assurance, referred to as Qualification, into daily implementation and operational activities. This approach ensures that quality assurance and project execution proceed concurrently, rather than as isolated, sequential steps. Under CIM, software features are developed, tested, evaluated, and refined in short, iterative cycles. Both technical teams and end users are actively involved throughout this process. Agile and iterative development models in healthcare IT demonstrate the benefits of short development cycles and user co-design[10].

This integrated methodology enhances both speed and adaptability, while significantly reducing the likelihood of post-implementation issues and user dissatisfaction. Comparative research showing agile/iterative approaches improve adaptability and reduce implementation failure in healthcare IT[11]. By aligning validation with ongoing development, CIM supports the delivery of systems that are better suited to the realities of healthcare operations.

Practical Tips for Applying CIM in Simultaneous Execution and QA:

1. Embed Quality Roles into Each Implementation Task

   Assign a QA point person (example: clinical lead, super-user, or QA engineer) to every development or configuration task, so validation begins alongside execution, not after it.
2. Use Micro-Testing Cycles for Every Feature Developed

   As each feature or module is developed (example: admission form, medication chart), run focused testing with real users or observers before moving on. This ensures alignment with workflows from day one.

3. Create "QA Windows" During Active Implementation
   Designate short, recurring blocks (example: at the end of each week) for the Implementation team to validate what's been built, offer improvements, and align with operational needs.
4. Involve End-Users in Acceptance and Usability Testing Early
   Don't wait until the system is "ready". Let selected users test small parts of the system regularly to provide practical insights.
5. Maintain a Live Defect and Feedback Register
   Use a transparent tool (example: a shared dashboard or feedback tracker) where issues are logged and status is visible to all. Make fixing issues part of the ongoing development process, not a post-launch task.

Common Mistakes and Fears

- Mistake: Treating QA as a Final Gate
  Teams may fear that early validation could slow down progress or distract from delivery timelines. This leads to late detection of usability or workflow mismatches, requiring rework and delaying go-live.
- Mistake: Involving QA Teams Only After Go-Live Planning Begins
  Managers may think involving quality experts too early will complicate early development phases. Systems will be built without real operational input, increasing resistance and failure rates later.
- Mistake: Skipping QA During Tight Schedules
  Under deadline pressure, managers may skip intermediate testing or user feedback. Quick fixes may backfire, leading to performance issues, user frustration, or even patient safety risks.
- Mistake: Limiting QA to Technical Validation Only
  Managers may focus solely on system functionality, fearing that subjective usability feedback is too vague or variable. Systems may technically work but fail to meet real user needs or fit into clinical workflows.

How to Address Mistakes and Fears with CIM

1. Normalize Quality as a Parallel Function
   CIM treats Qualification as a continuous, equal element alongside Implementation, eliminating the idea that QA is something "extra". This mindset helps remove the fear that QA slows down progress.
2. Use Observation to Integrate QA into Daily Workflows

Through the Observation element, CIM keeps implementation grounded in real-time monitoring. Observers can collect usability insights, track performance, and guide the qualification team to validate what matters most.

3. Build Mini-Feedback Loops

   Use short, regular feedback cycles that include both QA and implementation teams. This shows tangible progress and makes quality part of the delivery rhythm rather than a hurdle to cross later.

4. Empower Cross-Functional QA Involvement

   In CIM, quality is not just a technical concern, it's operational. Encourage super-users, clinical champions, and administrative leads to take active roles in reviewing functionality as it's developed.

5. Celebrate Continuous Improvement

   Reinforce the culture of "build, test, improve" by recognizing small improvements in usability and performance. This removes the fear of negative feedback and shifts the focus to progress and collaboration.

Further Reading

- *The Lean Startup*, Eric Ries
- *Lean Software Development: An Agile Toolkit*, Mary and Tom Poppendieck
- *Accelerate: The Science of Lean Software and DevOps*, Nicole Forsgren, Jez Humble, and Gene Kim
- *Lean Hospitals: Improving Quality, Patient Safety, and Employee Engagement*, Mark Graban
- *Safe Patients, Smart Hospitals*, Peter Pronovost and Eric Vohr
- *Toyota Kata: Managing People for Improvement, Adaptiveness and Superior Results*, Mike Rother.

Incremental and Adaptive Delivery

Incremental and adaptive delivery is a project management methodology in which solutions are developed, tested, and released in small, manageable components known as increments. Rather than deploying the entire system at once, each increment is designed to be functional, usable, and capable of providing value to users, even if it represents only a portion of the overall

Table 3.3 Continuous Quality Assurance in HIS Projects Using CIM

Category	*Key Concepts/Actions*	*Common Mistakes and Fears*	*CIM-Based Solutions and Practical Tips*
1. Philosophy of QA in HIS	- HIS is mission-critical and must evolve with user needs - Static QA at the end = costly rework - QA must be continuous and embedded from the start	- QA is treated as a final gate - Fear of slowing down progress - Belief that QA is only technical	- Normalize QA as parallel to implementation - Embrace "build, test, improve" culture - Promote shared ownership of quality among all stakeholders
2. Real-Time Integration (CIM Approach)	- CIM integrates QA ("Qualification") directly into daily tasks - QA and execution are simultaneous, not sequential - Validation happens in short feedback loops with end users	- QA delayed due to tight deadlines - QA seen as external to main workflow	- Assign QA roles to every task - Use short weekly QA windows - Micro-test each feature before moving forward
3. Stakeholder Involvement	- QA isn't just technical; it's clinical and operational - End-user feedback is essential early and often	- Fear of subjective or "vague" usability input - QA teams involved only at final stages	- Involve super-users and clinical leads in QA - Empower cross-functional teams - Normalize usability and operational validation as equal to technical testing

(*Continued*)

Table 3.3 (Continued) Continuous Quality Assurance in HIS Projects Using CIM

Category	*Key Concepts/Actions*	*Common Mistakes and Fears*	*CIM-Based Solutions and Practical Tips*
4. Feedback Infrastructure	- Live defect and feedback register - Transparent issue-tracking tools - Visible progress builds trust	- Ignoring or delaying response to feedback - Failing to close the loop, causing disengagement	- Maintain shared dashboards or trackers - Communicate how feedback leads to changes - Celebrate improvements (not just fixes)
5. Practical QA Activities	- Assign QA leads to implementation teams - Run micro-tests for each module (example admission form) - Hold post-implementation feedback workshops - Establish short QA cycles (weekly reviews) - Start acceptance testing early with real users	- Thinking feedback is disruptive or premature - Believing early feedback = delay - Limiting QA scope to "bugs" only	- Create small, fast feedback loops - Use Observation to inform Qualification team - Design workflows where testing and refinement are integrated into every step
6. Team Dynamics and Emotional Intelligence	- Conflicts may arise under pressure - Self-control and emotional resilience foster team stability - Shared ownership of QA builds team cohesion	- Fear of appearing weak in conflict - Avoiding tensions rather than channeling them constructively	- Foster psychological safety - Recognize stress as part of the process - Encourage calm leadership and active listening to keep focus on progress

system. Adaptation within this approach refers to the capacity to modify future increments in response to real-time feedback, emerging requirements, or changes within the hospital environment.

This methodology differs significantly from traditional "big bang" implementations, where the complete system is launched simultaneously after an extended period of design and development. Such large-scale deployments often result in elevated risk, user dissatisfaction, and misalignment between the system and organizational needs.

Socio-technical and implementation science literature recognizing healthcare IT implementation as a complex adaptive challenge[12]. This complexity arises from the diverse range of users, including clinicians, administrators, IT professionals, and management, the critical nature of hospital workflows, and the necessity to comply with evolving regulatory and operational requirements. Attempting to design and deliver the entire system in a single phase introduces significant risks and frequently results in the following challenges:

- Misalignment with actual hospital workflows.
- Resistance from end-users.
- Costly rework due to misinterpreted requirements.
- Downtime or disruptions in patient care.

While incremental and adaptive delivery reduces these risks by:

- Allowing users to validate system features early and continuously.
- Ensuring rapid value realization with each release.
- Enabling course correction based on real-world feedback.
- Increasing stakeholder confidence and engagement.
- Supporting training and change management in manageable chunks.

How the Core Interaction Model Supports Incremental and Adaptive Delivery

The Core Interaction Model (CIM) is inherently designed for incremental and adaptive delivery. Two of its defining characteristics, Agility and Incremental Development, form the backbone of its approach.

Agility in CIM

CIM promotes agility by creating continuous cycles of Observation, Implementation, and Qualification that operate in real-time. Unlike traditional linear methods, this allows the project team to:

- Respond quickly to new user needs, process changes, or external pressures.
- Integrate lessons learned immediately into the next development cycle.
- Shorten feedback loops between development and validation.

Incremental Development in CIM

In CIM, implementation is broken down into mini-projects or task forces that focus on specific modules (Group of functionalities) or single functionalities (example lab orders, medication workflows, and discharge summaries). Each increment is planned, developed, observed, validated, and improved, then followed by the next, allowing:

- Reduced scope complexity
- Quicker realization of benefits
- Progressive user adoption
- High flexibility without sacrificing structure

This structure is especially powerful in HIS environments, where end-user feedback is essential and where patient safety depends on gradual, well-tested deployment.

Practical Tips for Applying CIM in Incremental and Adaptive Delivery

1. Define Functional Increments Clearly
   Break down the HIS project into functional areas (example Patient Registration, Laboratory, and Billing) and plan each as a mini-project with its own Observation, Implementation, and Qualification cycle.
2. Use Real-World Testing Before Full Rollout
   Before deploying each increment across the hospital, test it in a controlled environment (example one ward or department) to refine based on user feedback.

3. Maintain a Flexible Implementation Roadmap
   Allow room to shift priorities based on urgent operational needs or feedback from earlier increments.
4. Track Incremental Progress Visibly
   Use dashboards or boards to show which modules are in progress, tested, deployed, or under review. This keeps all stakeholders aligned and motivated.
5. Collect and Act on Feedback Between Increments
   Schedule retrospective reviews with users and implementation teams after each increment to refine the next module or feature.

Common Mistakes and Fears in Incremental Delivery

- Mistake: Treating Each Increment Like a Mini Waterfall Project
  - Project teams may fear that small releases will still require rigid phases and signoffs, slowing agility. This negates the flexibility CIM is designed to offer and leads to slow, bureaucratic progress.
- Mistake: Neglecting Interdependencies Between Increments
  - Managers may worry that connecting increments too early will create errors, so they isolate features entirely. This creates siloed systems that don't integrate well and can cause rework.
- Mistake: Inconsistent User Involvement
  - Teams may believe that involving users in every cycle is too time-consuming. Reduced user input increases the risk of building features that are technically sound but clinically impractical.
- Mistake: Sticking to a Fixed Plan Despite Feedback
  - Managers may fear that changing plans makes them look unorganized. Ignoring real-time feedback undermines stakeholder trust and system effectiveness.

How to Address These Mistakes and Fears with CIM

1. Adopt Agile Mindset Through CIM's Agility Principle
   Reinforce that CIM is not about perfect planning, it's about responsive execution. Agility is a strength, not a sign of disorganization.
2. Build and Track Interdependencies in Observation and Implementation
   Use Observation to continuously monitor how each module interacts with others and ensure technical and clinical coherence.

Table 3.4 Incremental and Adaptive Delivery Using CIM

Category	*Key Concepts/ Actions*	*Common Mistakes and Fears*	*CIM-Based Solutions & Practical Tips*
Agility in CIM	Continuous cycles of Observation, Implementation, Qualification; short feedback loops	Slow reaction to changes, delayed validation	Real-time adaptation, integrated learning, fast delivery
Incremental Development in CIM	Implementation in mini-projects/task forces per module	Complexity if done all at once, slow user adoption	Reduced complexity, faster benefits, progressive adoption
Defining Functional Increments	Break HIS project into functional areas with own CIM cycle	Overgeneralization, lack of modular focus	Plan each increment with full CIM cycle for clarity and focus
Real-World Testing	Test each increment in a limited area before full rollout	Deploying untested modules leads to errors	Refine based on feedback from controlled environments
Flexible Roadmap	Allow dynamic prioritization of increments	Sticking to a fixed plan, ignoring new needs	Adjust roadmap based on feedback and urgency
Visible Progress Tracking	Use dashboards/ boards to track modules' progress	Lack of stakeholder clarity and motivation	Keep stakeholders aligned with visible status updates
Feedback Integration	Conduct retrospectives with users between increments	Loss of insights, misalignment with real needs	Use reviews to refine upcoming increments

3. Schedule Stakeholder Touchpoints in Observation Loops

   Plan recurring sessions where end-users review and test each increment as it's being developed, making engagement a habit, not an exception.

4. Celebrate Adaptation as a Success Factor
   Use early changes as proof that the system is evolving to fit real needs. Communicate changes clearly and show how user feedback is shaping the system.
5. Link Each Increment to Overall Goals via Qualification
   The Qualification phase ensures each increment aligns with the bigger picture – strategic goals, patient care improvements, or compliance needs.

Further Reading

- *Agile Estimating and Planning*, Mike Cohn
- *Agile Project Management with Kanban*, Eric Brechner
- *Making Things Happen*, Scott Berkun
- *Switch: How to Change Things When Change Is Hard*, Chip & Dan Heath
- *Accelerate: The Science of Lean Software and DevOps*, Nicole Forsgren, Jez Humble, and Gene Kim

Performance-Centric Progress Measurement

Evaluating success in Hospital Information System (HIS) requires more than simply meeting project timelines or adhering to budget constraints. Greater emphasis should be placed on system usability, clinical effectiveness, and operational efficiency. Research identifying usability, clinical outcomes, and workflow impact as core success indicators in EHR/HIS evaluation[13].

A performance-centric approach to progress measurement prioritizes the assessment of how effectively, usefully, and impactfully system components function in practice. Information systems success models emphasizing system quality, information quality, service quality, and net benefits rather than task completion[14]. This method moves beyond tracking task completion or milestone achievement.

In this context, success is determined not only by adherence to schedules or budgets, but by the tangible value and outcomes the system delivers to end users, patients, and the organization as a whole.

In HIS projects, this means monitoring how well the system:

- Improves clinical workflows
- Enhances user satisfaction
- Reduces operational bottlenecks
- Complies with regulatory standards
- Supports patient safety and care quality

Hospital Information System (HIS) operate in critical settings where the outcomes directly impact patient care, staff productivity, data accuracy, and adherence to regulatory standards. In these environments, the distinction between a successful and an unsuccessful implementation is significant.

Conventional methods of tracking project progress, such as measuring percentage completion or monitoring budget expenditure, frequently do not provide an accurate representation of the system's actual effectiveness in practice. Implementation science research showing discrepancy between project completion metrics and real-world system adoption/effectiveness[15].

Without performance-centric measurement, you risk:

- Deploying systems that are technically functional but clinically unusable.
- Missing usability issues that lead to low adoption.
- Overlooking integration problems that disrupt workflows.
- Delivering features that don't align with stakeholder expectations.
- Failing to detect system fatigue or inefficiencies post-go-live.

By focusing on performance, project teams can ensure the HIS delivers on its true purpose, enhancing healthcare delivery.

How the Core Interaction Model Supports Performance-Centric Progress

The Qualification component within the Core Interaction Model (CIM) is designed to integrate performance measurement across all stages of the project. Rather than serving as a final step, Qualification functions as an ongoing process. It systematically assesses the effectiveness, usability, and alignment of each Hospital Information System (HIS) module or feature with established clinical and organizational objectives.

Key Functions of Qualification in CIM

- Evaluating Outcomes: Measures actual outcomes of each module, not just functionality but also workflow integration, speed, accuracy, and user experience.
- Validating Project Objectives: Ensures that HIS features continuously align with original project goals and evolving needs.
- Continuous Testing and Learning: Applies real-time validation and feedback during each cycle of implementation, making adjustments on the fly.

CIM transforms performance tracking from a reporting task into a strategic feedback loop, linking every aspect of execution (Implementation) with outcome-driven insights (Qualification) and real-world monitoring (Observation).

Practical Tips for Performance-Centric Measurement Using CIM

1. Define Performance Metrics Early
   Collaborate with stakeholders to identify clear KPIs (example time to complete documentation, user satisfaction scores, and system response times) aligned with clinical and operational priorities.
2. Integrate Performance Checks into Every Increment
   After each module or feature is delivered, measure real-world performance immediately, not just technical success.
3. Use Dashboards to Visualize Key Metrics
   Create live dashboards that track performance indicators and make them accessible to stakeholders for transparency.
4. Schedule Ongoing Outcome Reviews
   Use the Qualification cycle to hold short, focused review sessions after each release to assess performance before moving forward.
5. Incorporate Qualitative Feedback
   Combine metrics with user stories, recorded sessions, or observation notes to capture both measurable and experiential performance.

Common Mistakes and Fears in Performance Measurement

- Mistake: Measuring Only Task Completion

  - Teams fear performance metrics will slow down delivery, so they only measure tasks completed. This gives a false sense of progress while ignoring whether the delivered features are actually useful.
- Mistake: Defining KPIs Too Late
  - Project managers may worry about committing to KPIs early and delay defining them. Without early KPI alignment, tracking becomes reactive and often irrelevant to actual goals.
- Mistake: Overemphasizing Quantitative Metrics
  - Teams may ignore qualitative insights, thinking they're too subjective. Critical usability or adoption issues are missed until they become serious problems.
- Mistake: Treating Performance Reviews as Formalities
  - Teams might fear honest feedback will delay the project, so reviews become box-checking exercises. This undermines the value of Qualification and leads to poor stakeholder trust.

How to Address These Mistakes and Fears with CIM

1. Start with Outcome-Centered Planning (Qualification + Observation)
   CIM encourages defining performance success criteria during the early Observation phase, so Qualification can start measuring real impact from the first increment.
2. Make Qualification Part of Daily Work, Not a Separate Step
   With CIM, quality and performance aren't deferred. They are built into each iteration, reducing the fear of delay and promoting a culture of continual improvement.
3. Use Real-World Testing to Validate Metrics
   Qualification in CIM integrates both data and user experience. Field testing and feedback sessions are built into each cycle, so insights are timely and actionable.
4. Promote Transparency Through Performance Dashboards
   Making performance visible builds trust and allows stakeholders to see their input influencing system success, encouraging ongoing collaboration.
5. Create a Safe Space for Honest Review
   The iterative nature of CIM means performance issues aren't viewed as failures. They're opportunities to adapt and evolve. This mindset removes fear from the equation.

Table 3.5 Performance-centric Progress Measurement Using CIM

Aspect	*Traditional Approach*	*Performance-Centric Approach (Enabled by CIM)*
Definition of Success	Timelines, budget, % task completion	Real-world outcomes: Usability, clinical effectiveness, operational efficiency
Focus Metrics	Technical completion, cost tracking	Clinical workflow improvement, user satisfaction, regulatory compliance, patient safety, and care quality
Risks Without Performance Focus	Technically functional but unusable systems, low adoption, misaligned features, and inefficiencies post-go-live	
CIM Contribution (Qualification)	N/A	Embedded, ongoing evaluation of each feature/module against real-world needs
Key Functions of CIM Qualification	N/A	- Evaluate outcomes (speed, UX, and workflow integration) - Validate evolving goals - Continuous testing and adjustment
Practical CIM-Based Strategies	N/A	- Define KPIs early with stakeholders - Measure performance after each increment - Use dashboards - Review outcomes regularly
Use of Feedback	Often ignored or delayed	Combine quantitative metrics with qualitative insights (user stories, observations)
Cultural Impact	Fear of delay, defensive mindset	Safe space for honest review, continuous learning, stakeholder trust, and iterative improvement

Further Reading

- Healy JC, Rodin D. *Health Information Systems: Architectures and Strategies.* World Health Organization; 2004.
- Friedman CP, Wyatt JC. *Evaluation Methods in Biomedical Informatics.* 2nd ed. Springer; 2006.
- Sittig DF. *Clinical Information Systems: Overcoming Barriers to Successful Implementation.* Jones & Bartlett Learning; 2008.
- Institute of Medicine. *Measuring the Impact of Interprofessional Education on Collaborative Practice and Patient Outcomes.* National Academies Press; 2015.
- Poister TH. *Managing and Measuring Performance in Public and Nonprofit Organizations: An Integrated Approach.* 2nd ed. Jossey-Bass; 2010.
- Berkun S. *Making Things Happen: Mastering Project Management.* O'Reilly Media; 2008.
- Derby E, Larsen D. *Agile Retrospectives: Making Good Teams Great.* Pragmatic Bookshelf; 2006.

Integrated Operations and Implementation

Hospital Information System (HIS) are not standalone software projects. They are embedded within the daily operations of hospitals. Integrated operations and implementation ensure that project activities, such as building, configuring, and testing the HIS, are closely aligned with the realities of clinical workflows, hospital processes, and routine tasks from the outset. Research emphasizing workflow integration as a key determinant of successful EHR implementation and sustainability[16].

Rather than considering the project as a separate entity with a single handover at completion, both project and operational activities develop concurrently. This approach allows for continuous adaptation and alignment between the system and hospital practices.

Implementing an HIS should not be viewed merely as the installation of a new software solution. Instead, integrated operations and implementation acknowledge it as a comprehensive operational transformation.

- Hospital workflows are adapted as the system is built which means real-time adaptation of system features to operational realities

- System functionalities are tuned based on real-world operations.
- Staff engagement is continuous, not limited to "training before go-live".
- Resistance from clinicians and hospital staff will be reduced because of Smooth transition for users, reducing fear and resistance, Increased ownership and buy-in from all departments, Early detection and resolution of operational issues

How the Core Interaction Model (CIM) Supports Integrated Operations and Implementation

In the Core Interaction Model, Integrated Operations and Implementation is not just a technique, it's the foundation.

There is no strict division between "project work" and "operational work". Observation, Implementation, and Qualification happen simultaneously and continuously within the live operational context.

Here's how CIM makes integration happen naturally:

Observation Keeps the Project Grounded in Reality

- Ongoing monitoring ensures that system development is always aligned with the current operational environment.
- Feedback and needs are gathered directly from frontline staff during day-to-day work, not just through isolated workshops.

Implementation Progresses Within Real Operations

- New functionalities are developed, tested, and adapted while operations continue.
- Mini-go-lives (example rolling out modules department-by-department) ensure that HIS becomes a natural extension of how staff already work.

Qualification Ensures Immediate Validation

- System features are evaluated against actual clinical workflows, not just theoretical scenarios.
- Quality checks and user acceptance happen dynamically, avoiding major surprises at final go-live.

Through this constant cycle, CIM merges projects and operations into a single living, evolving environment, rather than treating them as separate worlds.

Practical Tips for Achieving Integrated Operations and Implementation with CIM

1. Embed Implementation Teams Within Hospital Departments: Instead of working separately, assign project team members (like IT leads or super-users) directly to clinical and administrative units during implementation.
2. Use Rolling Go-Lives Rather Than a Single Launch Event: Deploy the HIS in phases across different departments, services, or processes, testing integration with daily operations as you go.
3. Maintain Continuous Feedback Mechanisms from Day 1: Set up systems (dashboards, feedback portals, open forums) where users can provide operational feedback throughout implementation, not just during training.
4. Adapt Training to Real-Time Workflow Changes: As the system and workflows evolve together, training should be updated and delivered incrementally alongside each operational change.
5. Create Joint Operational and Project Teams: Ensure every task force or committee has both project staff (IT, consultants) and operational staff (nurses, doctors, and admin) represented.

Common Mistakes and Fears in Integration

- Mistake: Treating Implementation and Operations as Two Separate Worlds
  - Managers may fear that involving operational teams will slow down technical development. The result is systems that don't fit real workflows, leading to chaos after go-live.
- Mistake: Only Involving Operations at the End
  - Project leaders may believe it's "more efficient" to finish system development before involving end-users heavily. Leads to massive redesign needs and late-stage resistance.

Table 3.6 Integrated Operations and Implementation Using CIM

Category	*Key Concepts/ Actions*	*Common Mistakes and Fears*	*CIM-Based Solutions and Practical Tips*
Foundational Integration	- No separation between project and operations - Observation, Implementation, and Qualification happen simultaneously	- Belief that involving operations slows progress - Viewing project and operations as separate domains	- Treat all project work as embedded in live operations - Align system changes with ongoing workflow dynamics
Observation	- Continuous feedback from frontline staff - Monitoring based on real-time use, not workshops	- Only involving users during requirement-gathering or late phases	- Use dashboards, forums, or portals from Day 1 - Create joint review points during real operations
Implementation	- Features rolled out during daily operations - Mini-go-lives ensure adaptation to each environment	- Delaying operations involvement until final go-live - Assuming system fit without field testing	- Use rolling go-lives department-by-department - Assign IT leads/ super-users within clinical units
Qualification	- Validation against real clinical workflows - Quality and usability checked in real-time	- Thinking testing is a final phase task - Ignoring user experience until go-live	- Continuously evaluate and refine features post-deployment - Adapt training and documentation to evolving workflows

(*Continued*)

Table 3.6 (Continued) Integrated Operations and Implementation Using CIM

Category	*Key Concepts/ Actions*	*Common Mistakes and Fears*	*CIM-Based Solutions and Practical Tips*
Cross-Functional Teams	- Project + operational staff in same committees/ task forces	- Project team works in isolation - Operational staff only consulted for training	- Form integrated teams from project start - Involve doctors, nurses, and admins directly in design and deployment
Training and Change Management	- Training evolves with workflow changes - Delivered incrementally during implementation	- Rigid, one-time training sessions - Mismatch between training and actual system usage	- Deliver modular training updates with each rollout - Align sessions with evolving workflows
Cultural Alignment & Readiness	- HIS adapts to staff, not vice versa - Readiness = operational stability, not technical go-live	- Underestimating impact on frontline work - Expecting users to "just adjust"	- Redefine success as smooth workflow + stable adoption - Normalize disruption as part of progress
Momentum Building	- Early success stories improve adoption	- Fear of failure leads to delay in feedback loops or change	- Celebrate and share operational wins (example time saved, error reduced) - Build trust by showing tangible improvements early
Expectation Management	- Transparent communication about integration process	- Fear that transparency may create resistance	- Set leadership expectations early - Communicate that system + operations evolve together

- Mistake: Underestimating Operational Disruption Risks
  - Project teams may underestimate how deeply HIS affects frontline tasks, thinking that disruption is temporary and users will "get used to it". Prolonged productivity drops, clinician burnout, and poor system adoption.

How to Address Mistakes and Fears with CIM

1. Normalize Cross-Participation Through Observation and Implementation
   Project activities must always involve operational stakeholders. CIM's structure demands constant Observation tied to real work realities, not abstract development.
2. Redefine Progress to Include Operational Readiness
   Success isn't just coding modules, it's ensuring that workflows are functioning smoothly with each new increment.
3. Use Rolling Integration and Testing
   Introduce new functionalities gradually into daily operations. Adapt and optimize workflows continuously alongside technical builds.
4. Proactively Manage Expectations and Communication
   Set clear expectations with hospital leadership: System and operations will evolve together, and some disruption is normal and planned for, but it's minimized through integration.
5. Celebrate Early Operational Wins
   Acknowledge small successes where new functionalities improve daily tasks, building momentum and staff confidence.

Further Reading

- *Improving Outcomes with Clinical Decision Support:* An Implementer's Guide, edited by Jerry Osheroff et al.
- *Integrated Clinical Systems: A Guide to Implementation and Operation*, Michael E. Frisina
- *The Design, Implementation, and Evaluation of Health Information Systems*, edited by Jytte Brender McNair
- *Beyond Implementation: A Prescription for Lasting EMR Adoption*, Heather Haugen & Jeffrey Didier
- *The Fifth Discipline: The Art & Practice of The Learning Organization*, Peter M. Senge

- *Sociotechnical Theory for Health Information Systems Implementation*, Borycki & Kushniruk

Domain-Centered Role Assignment

It is not necessary for every individual to serve as a project manager; however, it is essential that each person understands their specific role and how it contributes to the success of the Health Information System (HIS). Project governance and healthcare IT implementation literature emphasizing role clarity and responsibility definition as critical success factors[17].

The principle of Domain-Centered Role Assignment ensures that all participants in an HIS implementation project or operation, whether from clinical, administrative, IT, or vendor backgrounds, are assigned responsibilities that align with their particular areas of expertise. Instead of requiring all team members to perform every task, this approach allows each group to concentrate on duties that correspond to their professional strengths and core responsibilities.

For example:

- Clinicians focus on validating clinical workflows and user needs.
- IT specialists focus on configuring and technically implementing the system.
- Quality teams focus on ensuring usability, compliance, and process integration.
- Project managers focus on coordination, planning, and communication across groups.

In a domain-centered approach, assigning clear ownership of roles is essential to ensure that all critical areas receive appropriate attention. This structure allows decisions to be made by individuals who possess the necessary expertise, thereby enhancing the quality and effectiveness of outcomes. Interprofessional collaboration and distributed leadership literature showing improved decision quality when authority aligns with expertise[18].

As teams progress through stages of development, the ability to manage conflicts and maintain constructive relationships becomes crucial. When team members successfully address disagreements and establish mutual trust and understanding, a foundation of ethical maturity is formed. Organizational ethics and psychological safety literature emphasizing trust, mutual respect, and conflict resolution in high-reliability healthcare organizations[19]. At this stage, significant effort has been dedicated to resolving conflicts, fostering healthy interactions, and clearly defining the roles and responsibilities within the group.

Health Information System (HIS) projects are highly complex and influence nearly every aspect of a hospital's operations. Their scope extends from direct patient care to administrative functions such as billing, pharmacy, laboratory services, and overall management. In the absence of well-defined, domain-specific roles, critical areas may be neglected, and the effectiveness of the project can be compromised, so:

- Teams get overwhelmed trying to cover areas they don't fully understand.
- Miscommunication and mistakes increase because decisions are made by the wrong stakeholders.
- Gaps emerge in critical areas like clinical usability, IT integration, and regulatory compliance.
- Staff become frustrated and disengaged when they are asked to perform outside their skill sets.

Domain-centered role assignment ensures:

- Expertise is properly leveraged across all phases.
- Collaboration is structured, efficient, and productive.
- Accountability is clear, avoiding confusion and finger-pointing.
- System quality and operational safety are maintained.

How the Core Interaction Model (CIM) Supports Domain-Centered Role Assignment:

The Core Interaction Model (CIM) is naturally built around differentiating stakeholder roles into three core functions

In CIM, no stakeholder is forced to act outside their expertise unnecessarily. Instead, each group plays its most effective role, contributing to real-time feedback loops, development cycles, and continuous quality assurance without role confusion.

By clearly defining roles around Observation, Implementation, and Qualification, CIM:

- Reduces redundancy
- Prevents critical gaps in system development and validation
- Increases efficiency and project velocity
- Strengthens ownership and responsibility for project outcomes

Practical Tips for Applying Domain-Centered Role Assignment with CIM:

1. Map Stakeholders to Domains Early
   During project initiation, create a matrix mapping stakeholders to their domain areas (example clinical validation, technical implementation, and operational feedback).
2. Assign Clear Responsibilities Within CIM Elements
   Assign specific individuals or teams as responsible for Observation (needs analysis), Implementation (building/configuration), and Qualification (testing/validation).
3. Avoid Overlapping or Confusing Roles
   Ensure that while collaboration is encouraged, responsibility for each domain is clear to avoid misunderstandings.
4. Use RACI Matrices (Responsible, Accountable, Consulted, and Informed)
   Define who is responsible for each task across Observation, Implementation, and Qualification. Update RACI charts as the project evolves.
5. Align Communications with Roles
   Tailor meetings, updates, and issue escalations according to domain responsibilities. Clinical updates should go to clinical leads; technical issues to IT; regulatory updates to quality managers.

Common Mistakes and Fears in Role Assignment

- Mistake: Expecting "All-Rounders" to Cover All Areas
  - Managers may fear losing control if too much specialization occurs, leading them to ask individuals to wear multiple hats. Staff become overloaded, critical areas are neglected, and errors multiply.
- Mistake: Underestimating the Need for Specialized Validation
  - Project leaders may think general IT testing is enough without clinical validation. Clinical workflows fail because the system is technically correct but operationally unusable.

Table 3.7 Domain-Centered Role Assignment Using CIM

CIM Element	*Who (Typical Roles)*	*Focus*
Observation	Clinical champions, medical informatics specialists, and IT liaisons	Identifying needs, gathering feedback, and monitoring operations
Implementation	IT teams, software developers, and configuration specialists	Building, configuring, integrating, and technically testing system features
Qualification	Quality assurance teams, clinical validators, and regulatory specialists	Testing usability, compliance, and validating workflows and system outcomes

- Mistake: Assuming Domains Are Static Throughout the Project
  - Managers may believe initial role assignments are final. As the project evolves, new roles or additional responsibilities emerge – but without updates, critical areas are missed.
- Mistake: Poor Communication Across Domains
  - Leaders may fear overcomplicating communications, resulting in not connecting Observation, Implementation, and Qualification groups properly. Misalignment between what is built, what is needed, and what is validated.

How to Address These Mistakes and Fears with CIM

1. Anchor Every Role in a Core Function (Observation, Implementation, and Qualification)

   Reiterate that domain-specific roles are part of the natural structure of CIM, not additional bureaucracy.
2. Designate Domain Leads and Liaison Points

   Appoint leads for each major function who ensure their domain's interests are consistently represented throughout the project.
3. Maintain Agile Role Mapping

   Review and adjust role assignments regularly during Observation cycles as hospital needs and project complexity evolve.
4. Encourage Cross-Functional Communication Without Role Confusion

   Facilitate regular cross-functional meetings where domain experts share updates, but each remains responsible only for their expertise.

5. Celebrate Domain-Specific Wins
   Recognize successes where specialized teams (example nursing champions, IT developers, and QA validators) contribute critical improvements. This strengthens role ownership and motivation.

Further Reading

- *Healthcare Information Systems: A Practical Approach for HealthCare Management*, Karen A. Wager, Frances Wickham Lee, and John P. Glaser
- *Information Systems for Healthcare Management*, Gerald Glandon, Detlev H. Smaltz, and Donna J. Slovensky
- *Biomedical Informatics: Computer Applications in HealthCare and Biomedicine*, Edward H. Shortliffe, James J. Cimino
- *The Project Manager's Guide to Health Information Technology Implementation*, Susan M. Houston, Denise E. Beaulieu
- *Team of Teams: New Rules of Engagement for a Complex World*, General Stanley McChrystal
- *Cognitive Work Analysis: Toward Safe, Productive, and Healthy Computer-Based Work*, Kim Vicente

Cultural Transformation as a Strategic Objective

Technology adoption within the healthcare sector is significantly shaped by the prevailing culture and mindset of an organization. These factors play a critical role in determining how effectively new systems and innovations are integrated into daily operations.

Cultural transformation, particularly in the context of implementing and operating Hospital Information System (HIS), involves a deliberate shift in the mindset, attitudes, behaviors, and daily practices of both hospital staff and leadership. Organizational change literature in healthcare IT emphasizing behavioral change, leadership engagement, and transformation of work practices during EHR implementation[20]. The objective is to ensure that technology is regarded as an integral and valuable component of healthcare delivery, rather than as an external or disruptive element.

This transformation extends beyond the technical installation of a system. It requires a fundamental change in how individuals perceive, interact with, and depend on digital solutions to enhance patient care and improve operational efficiency.

In summary, the success of an HIS project relies not only on technological advancement but also on cultural evolution within the organization. Cultural transformation is essential as a strategic objective; without it, even the most well-designed HIS may fail to achieve its intended outcomes.

Why Is Cultural Transformation Critical in Hospital Information System (HIS) Projects?

Hospital staff, including doctors, nurses, administrators, and IT teams, already operate under high stress, tight schedules, and deeply ingrained workflows. Introducing a new HIS impacts everything they do, and naturally triggers:

- Fear of change
- Resistance to new processes
- Skepticism toward digital tools
- Anxiety over errors or system failures
- Nostalgia for "the old ways"

If cultural transformation is not treated as a core, strategic objective:

- Adoption will be half-hearted at best.
- System usage will be inconsistent or even resisted.
- Workarounds and "shadow systems" (example paper records) will emerge.
- Clinical and operational goals will not be achieved, despite technical success.

A strong cultural transformation ensures:

- Staff see HIS as an enabler, not an obstacle.
- Technology becomes integrated naturally into clinical practice.
- Engagement, learning, and innovation flourish around the system.
- Patient care and hospital performance improve sustainably.

How the Core Interaction Model (CIM) Supports Cultural Transformation:

The CIM is inherently designed to promote cultural transformation, even though it doesn't make it a separate "task" or "phase".

Instead, CIM implicitly supports cultural change through its core structure of continuous stakeholder engagement, feedback loops, and cross-functional collaboration.

Here's how:

Continuous Stakeholder Engagement

- Observation teams (clinical champions, IT liaisons) maintain a constant connection with staff, addressing concerns and building trust over time.
- Staff don't just receive information, they co-create the system and feel ownership from the start.

Real-Time Feedback Loops

- The ability for staff to see their feedback acted upon quickly builds confidence in the system and in leadership.
- Positive reinforcement shows that change is not top-down but responsive and inclusive.

Cross-Functional Collaboration

- Implementation is not isolated to IT or administration, all departments participate actively, reinforcing the message that the HIS is a shared responsibility and opportunity.
- Collaboration across clinical, technical, and administrative boundaries encourages a more open, adaptive, and innovative culture.

Through these mechanisms, CIM naturally drives cultural transformation without forcing it unnaturally or relying only on formal "change management programs".

Practical Tips for Enabling Cultural Transformation Using CIM:

1. Involve Influencers Early
   Identify and engage respected clinical, administrative, and IT leaders as role models (example "change champions") to drive positive attitudes toward the HIS.
2. Show Quick Wins Publicly
   Celebrate early successes, such as faster patient admissions, reduced medication errors, or improved data access, making the system's value visible to everyone.
3. Use Regular, Two-Way Communication Channels
   Keep dialogue open between project teams and staff. Regularly update users on changes made based on their feedback.
4. Normalize Adaptation and Learning
   Frame system tweaks, workflow changes, and iterations as normal parts of the journey, not as "failures", to build a growth mindset.
5. Support Emotional Responses to Change
   Acknowledge that fear, skepticism, and frustration are normal, and create safe spaces (forums, meetings) for staff to express concerns and get support.

Common Mistakes and Fears in Cultural Transformation

- Mistake: Assuming Culture Will Change Automatically
  - Managers may fear that talking too much about change will cause resistance, so they stay silent. Staff fill the silence with rumors, fear, and negativity.
- Mistake: Over-Focusing on Technical Training
  - Project leaders may believe that teaching the system's features is enough to ensure adoption. Staff understand how to use the system but not why, leading to disengagement.
- Mistake: Ignoring Emotional Responses
  - Managers may avoid discussing emotions, seeing them as unprofessional or outside project scope. Anxiety, resentment, and burnout grow unaddressed.
- Mistake: Treating Culture Change as a One-Time Event
  - Leaders may think that a few training sessions or newsletters will "fix" resistance permanently. Culture transformation needs continuous nurturing, not a one-off campaign.

Table 3.8 Cultural Transformation with CIM

Category	*Key Concepts/ Actions*	*Common Mistakes and Fears*	*CIM-Based Solutions and Practical Tips*
Continuous Stakeholder Engagement	- Clinical champions and IT liaisons stay connected with staff - Staff co-create the system, building ownership	- Assuming culture will change automatically - Fear of over communicating change	- Integrate cultural topics into regular Observation - Involve influencers early - Use two-way communication channels
Real-Time Feedback Loops	- Staff see their feedback quickly acted upon - Builds trust and inclusion	- Ignoring emotional responses - Believing "just technical training" is enough	- Share stories of how feedback improved the system - Frame changes as adaptation, not failure - Publicly celebrate early wins and staff contributions
Cross-Functional Collaboration	- All departments (clinical, admin, and IT) collaborate - HIS becomes a shared responsibility	- Treating cultural transformation as a one-time event - Thinking technical rollout alone will foster buy-in	- Maintain long-term visibility of champions - Keep culture messaging alive post go-live - Create mixed teams for ongoing improvement
Emotional Support and Mindset	- Acknowledge skepticism and fear as normal - Normalize learning and change as part of growth	- Avoiding discussions on emotional impact - Viewing resistance as failure	- Provide safe forums for emotional expression - Accept resistance and manage through dialogue - Celebrate adaptability and curiosity alongside system compliance

How to Address These Mistakes and Fears with CIM

1. Integrate Culture Messaging into Observation and Communication
   Make cultural adaptation a standing agenda item during all Observation activities (example feedback meetings, user groups).
2. Focus on Storytelling Through Feedback Loops
   Share real examples of how user feedback led to system improvements and operational benefits.
3. Celebrate Adaptability, Not Just Compliance
   Reward departments and teams not just for using the system correctly, but for finding better ways to integrate it into workflows.
4. Maintain Long-Term Cultural Reinforcement
   Keep leadership and project champions visible after initial go-live. Encourage them to share ongoing progress stories, lessons learned, and continuous improvements.
5. Accept and Normalize Resistance as Part of the Process
   Rather than fighting resistance, anticipate it, respect it, and manage it through continuous dialogue and evidence of benefits.

Further Reading

- *Digital Transformation and Healthcare: Frameworks and Roadmaps*, Nilmini Wickramasinghe
- *Leading Digital: Turning Technology into Business Transformation*, George Westerman, Didier Bonnet, and Andrew McAfee
- *The Heart of Change: Real-Life Stories of How People Change Their Organizations*, John Kotter & Dan Cohen
- *An Everyone Culture: Becoming a Deliberately Developmental Organization*, Robert Kegan & Lisa Lahey

Resilience and Responsiveness to Change

Research describing healthcare as a dynamic, policy-driven, technology-intensive environment requiring adaptive governance and flexible implementation strategies[21]. Healthcare regulations, technologies, and hospital priorities are subject to rapid change. It is essential that projects in this environment are able to adapt efficiently. The concept of resilience in project management encompasses the capacity of both the project and its stakeholders to endure challenges, adjust to unforeseen disruptions, and recover promptly, all while maintaining focus and momentum. Project resilience theory defining resilience as the capability to absorb shocks, adapt, and recover while sustaining project objectives[22].

Responsiveness to change involves the ability to quickly identify, evaluate, and respond to shifting circumstances. Digital health governance and regulatory science literature identifying clinical practice evolution, operational pressures, compliance demands, and technological innovation as core drivers of change[23].

Within Hospital Information System (HIS) projects, resilience and responsiveness are not merely advantageous; they are fundamental attributes necessary for success. High-reliability organization (HRO) theory and health IT safety research emphasizing resilience as essential in safety-critical healthcare systems[24].

Why Resilience and Responsiveness Are Crucial in HIS Projects

Hospital Information System (HIS) operate in dynamic, high-stakes environments. During HIS implementation, change is inevitable:

- New hospital policies may emerge.
- Clinical workflows may shift due to regulatory updates.
- Staff turnover may impact user training.
- External pressures like pandemics or accreditation demands can reshape priorities overnight.

Without resilience and responsiveness:

- Projects get stuck trying to follow outdated plans.
- Delays multiply as teams scramble to react.
- Staff lose confidence in leadership and the system.
- The system risks becoming outdated before it is even fully implemented.

With strong resilience and responsiveness:

- Projects stay aligned with real-world needs.
- Teams adjust workflows and system features proactively.

- Stakeholder trust and satisfaction increase.
- Go-live happens with a system that fits the current, evolving hospital reality.

How the Core Interaction Model (CIM) Supports Resilience and Responsiveness:

The CIM is built for resilience and responsiveness.

Unlike rigid project structures, CIM thrives on dynamic feedback loops and Observation-Driven Analysis, two elements that make real-time adaptation possible and sustainable.

Dynamic Feedback Loops

- CIM ensures that users, stakeholders, and implementation teams are in constant two-way communication.
- Observers gather feedback continuously, and responses are implemented quickly – not months later.
- This real-time dialogue makes the system agile and the project naturally adaptive.

Observation-Driven Analysis

- CIM empowers project teams to analyze changing needs continuously, not just at the beginning or in post-mortem reviews.
- Observers are embedded in operational workflows, allowing them to detect early warning signs of disruption or emerging needs.
- Analysis is not static, it evolves with the environment, keeping the project aligned without requiring major resets.

Through these mechanisms, CIM institutionalizes resilience and responsiveness rather than leaving them to chance.

Practical Tips for Building Resilience and Responsiveness with CIM

1. Conduct Ongoing Environmental Scanning

   Train observers to regularly assess external and internal factors (regulations, staffing changes, and hospital policies) that could affect the project.

2. Update Priorities Regularly
   Hold monthly or bi-monthly mini-retrospectives to review and, if needed, reprioritize tasks and features based on new realities.
3. Empower Teams to Make Quick Adjustments
   Decentralize small decisions (example adjusting a form field or updating a workflow) so frontline teams can react swiftly without heavy bureaucratic overhead.
4. Build Flexibility into the Project Plan
   Use flexible timelines and contingency buffers in the project schedule to absorb unexpected changes without triggering panic.
5. Celebrate Adaptability as a Strength
   Recognize teams or individuals who identify and respond effectively to changes, reinforcing the value of resilience.

Common Mistakes and Fears in Resilience and Change Responsiveness

- Mistake: Treating Change as an Exception
  - Leaders may fear that acknowledging frequent change will make the project seem out of control. Change gets hidden or ignored until it causes a crisis.
- Mistake: Sticking Rigidly to the Original Plan
  - Project teams may fear that adapting will be seen as "failing to plan properly". Teams waste resources trying to execute plans that no longer make sense.
- Mistake: Over-Controlling Adjustments
  - Leaders may fear losing authority if teams adjust workflows or features on their own. Valuable, time-sensitive adjustments are delayed or blocked.
- Mistake: Treating Feedback as Low Priority
  - Managers may think feedback gathering is "nice to have" rather than essential. Opportunities for early course correction are lost.

How to Address These Mistakes and Fears with CIM

1. Normalize Change as a Standard Process Through Dynamic Feedback Loops
   Use CIM's dynamic feedback mechanisms to show that change is not a threat. It's expected, welcomed, and managed systematically.

Table 3.9 Resilience and Responsiveness with CIM

Category	*Key Concepts/ Actions*	*Common Mistakes and Fears*	*CIM-Based Solutions and Practical Tips*
Dynamic Feedback Loops	- Continuous two-way communication - Feedback is gathered and acted on in real-time - Agile, adaptive environment	- Treating change as an exception - Viewing feedback as non-essential	- Normalize change through dynamic feedback - Treat feedback as a priority input - Celebrate adaptability as a core value
Observation-Driven Analysis	- Embedded observers analyze shifting needs - Continuous analysis replaces one-time reviews - Early detection of disruptions	- Sticking rigidly to original plans - Delaying action until post-crisis	- Link decisions to real-time observation - Use Observation reports to adjust without overhauls
Empowered Teams	- Decentralize small decisions for faster response - Teams adjust forms, workflows, and tasks on the ground	- Over-controlling adjustments - Fear of losing authority or consistency	- Let teams handle tactical changes - Keep strategic alignment via regular Observation checkpoints
Flexible Project Planning	- Use contingency buffers and rolling priorities - Schedule regular retrospectives (example monthly) - Reprioritize based on evolving context	- Viewing plan changes as failure - Fearing that adaptation shows poor initial planning	- Build in flexibility from the start - Update priorities regularly with input from Observation
Leadership Engagement	- Leaders stay updated on real-time insights - Reward proactive teams - Promote change-readiness culture	- Feedback seen as "optional" - Leadership disconnected from day-to-day adaptation	- Make Observation summaries visible to leaders - Acknowledge teams that spot and respond to change early

2. Link Adaptation Decisions to Observation-Driven Analysis
   Make it clear that changes are based on structured observation, not emotional reactions. This protects decision-making credibility.
3. Decentralize Tactical Changes While Keeping Strategic Alignment
   Allow teams to make day-to-day adjustments while keeping big-picture goals stable and visible through regular Observation reports.
4. Reward Early Identification of Risks and Opportunities
   Highlight teams that spot emerging issues early and act on them. This shifts the culture toward proactive, resilient thinking.
5. Keep Leadership Actively Involved in Change Monitoring
   Ensure leadership reviews real-time Observation summaries, keeping top management tuned into the reality on the ground.

Further Reading

- *Resilience: Hard-Won Wisdom for Living a Better Life*, Eric Greitens
- *Leadership on the Line: Staying Alive Through the Dangers of Leading*, Ronald Heifetz & Marty Linsky
- *Change Healthcare: Why Our Systems Are Failing and How to Fix Them*, David B. Nash
- *Managing the Unmanageable: Rules, Tools, and Insights for Managing Software People and Teams*, Mickey W. Mantle & Ron Lichty

Unified, Cross-Functional Team Collaboration

Initiating work as a group marks a significant step forward, but true team success depends on effective collaboration. Healthcare team performance literature demonstrating that interprofessional collaboration, conflict management, and defined team structures are central to implementation success[25]. Essential aspects of team management include addressing conflicts among members, establishing consistent team dynamics, and ensuring that responsibilities are carried out accurately.

Interprofessional collaboration research linking multidisciplinary integration to improved system adoption and organizational performance[26]. Unified, cross-functional collaboration involves professionals from diverse backgrounds, such as clinical, administrative, technical, and project management, working together as a single, integrated team throughout the Health Information System (HIS) implementation process.

This approach stands in contrast to working in isolated silos, where, for example, the IT department develops the system independently, clinical staff provide feedback only after implementation, and administrators remain uninformed. Instead, unified collaboration requires all key participants to engage actively from the outset through to project completion. This ensures shared ownership, a collective understanding of the system, and alignment toward common objectives.

Cross-functional teams are not just about coordination, they are about co-creation:

- Clinicians shape workflows and ensure usability.
- IT staff ensure technical feasibility and system performance.
- Administrative teams address compliance, billing, and operational requirements.
- Project managers orchestrate the effort and keep alignment.

HIS projects impact every corner of a hospital, meaning no single group has all the knowledge or authority needed for success.

Without unified collaboration:

- Systems are designed without clinical usability in mind.
- Technical decisions are made without understanding operational impacts.
- Administrative compliance risks are overlooked.
- Silos create frustration, misunderstandings, and resistance.

When unified, cross-functional collaboration is strong:

- Issues are caught early from multiple angles (technical, clinical, and operational).
- Solutions are co-designed, not forced onto users.
- Trust and teamwork increase across departments.
- Change management becomes smoother because everyone is involved from the beginning.

NOTE:

Close communication between different organizational levels, including management, clinicians, and information technology staff, is crucial for the successful implementation of a Hospital Information System (HIS). Ensuring this connection with specialized individuals who can act as intermediaries between clinicians and the information management and technology sector is necessary. Specialists in health information technology take on the responsibility of facilitating information flow and work processes, solving problems, and ensuring that everyone understands the new system. This not only provides benefits like better information flow and support but also strengthens relationships between management, technology staff, and clinicians.

At the outset of a project within various hospital departments, it is essential to involve all relevant stakeholders and ensure a comprehensive understanding of concepts such as software design and implementation. User-centered design and participatory implementation research in healthcare IT demonstrating early user testing improves usability and adoption. Human-centered design frameworks in digital health emphasizing clinician and patient co-design for meaningful system fit[27]. This approach helps confirm that the system will address the requirements of both specialists and patients.

Risk assessment during this phase should include identifying which individuals are likely to continue supporting the project. Those who do not recognize the value of the project are unlikely to contribute to its ongoing success. As a result, support for the project may not be uniform across all healthcare providers. Some individuals may be resistant, while others may possess considerable organizational influence that could affect the project's progress.

To promote sustained support, it is important to engage stakeholders early and clearly define the value of the system. Establishing this understanding from the beginning helps ensure continued commitment throughout the project's duration.

NOTE:

Nurses' resistance in these conditions will affect the support of doctors who collaborate with them. To attract the participation of everyone in the healthcare center, it is necessary for one of the staff members to explain the system's benefits directly and clarify the roles for the others.

The "project implementation team" can be different from the "system selection team". The system selection team is more focused on units and sections, while the implementation team will combine technical experts and clinicians.

How the Core Interaction Model (CIM) Supports Cross-Functional Collaboration

The Core Interaction Model (CIM) integrates collaboration at its core.

Rather than organizing the project into isolated technical or functional streams, CIM builds teams around Observation, Implementation, and Qualification, embedding collaboration across all phases.

Here's how CIM enables this:

Collaborative and Cross-Functional Teams in CIM

- Observation teams include clinical champions, administrative leaders, and IT liaisons, gathering feedback across domains.
- Implementation teams mix developers, system analysts, and operational representatives to ensure real-world applicability during development.
- Qualification teams involve quality specialists, end-user testers, compliance officers, and department heads.

In CIM, no stage is owned by one domain alone, multiple perspectives are embedded into each activity.

This leads to better system design, faster issue resolution, and stronger project resilience.

Practical Tips for Building Cross-Functional Collaboration with CIM

1. Form Integrated Teams from the Start
   Don't create "technical teams" and "clinical teams" separately. Instead, assign members from different areas to shared working groups aligned with Observation, Implementation, and Qualification activities.
2. Facilitate Joint Problem-Solving Sessions
   When issues arise, bring clinicians, IT, and administrative experts into the same room to find solutions together rather than handing problems off between silos.
3. Rotate Roles in Observation and Feedback Activities
   Allow different stakeholders (clinical, IT, admin) to lead feedback sessions occasionally, promoting empathy and shared understanding.
4. Use Shared Tools and Dashboards
   Implement transparent project management tools where all team members can track progress, issues, and changes, fostering shared ownership.
5. Recognize and Celebrate Team Wins
   Acknowledge achievements that cross domains (example IT helping clinical staff solve workflow issues or clinicians validating technical improvements).

Common Mistakes and Fears in Cross-Functional Collaboration

- Mistake: Treating Collaboration as "Nice to Have"
  - Leaders may fear that collaborative processes will slow things down. Silos deepen, misunderstandings multiply, and resistance grows.
- Mistake: Overloading Certain Domains
  - Project managers may fear involving clinical staff too much will distract them from patient care, so they exclude them from design and decision-making. The system is developed without frontline realities in mind, causing poor adoption.
- Mistake: Allowing Dominance by One Group (example IT or Management)
  - Leaders may fear conflict if multiple domains challenge each other openly, so they let one group dominate. Critical perspectives are lost, and the final product becomes unbalanced.

Table 3.10 Cross-Functional Collaboration with CIM

Category	*Key Concepts/Actions*	*Common Mistakes and Fears*	*CIM-Based Solutions and Practical Tips*
Team Structure & Roles	- Observation, Implementation, and Qualification teams include clinical, admin, and IT stakeholders - No activity is owned by a single domain	- Treating collaboration as "nice to have" - Assuming collaboration will happen naturally	- Form integrated, cross-domain teams from the beginning - Structure activities to mandate participation from all domains
Joint Problem Solving	- Mixed teams address issues together in real-time - Barriers between clinical, technical, and admin teams are broken down	- Overloading some domains (example clinicians left out to "focus on care") - Teams work in silos	- Facilitate joint resolution sessions - Use shared dashboards and tools visible to all roles
Shared Ownership and Leadership	- Rotate roles in Observation and feedback - Celebrate shared wins that span across domains	- Allowing one group (example IT or management) to dominate - Fear of cross-domain conflicts	- Distribute leadership across clinical, IT, and admin teams - Coach early collaborative interactions to ensure balanced contribution
Culture of Collaboration	- Collaboration is embedded, not optional - Teams are built around shared goals (example patient care, efficiency), not just technical delivery	- Believing that forming a team is enough - Not celebrating cross-functional success	- Use facilitators to guide early collaboration - Measure and reward cross-domain teamwork - Emphasize shared language and hospital-wide mission

- Mistake: Assuming Collaboration Will Happen Naturally
  - Teams may assume that just putting people together ensures collaboration. Without structured facilitation, teams drift into parallel work rather than true integration.

How to Address These Mistakes and Fears with CIM

1. Structure Cross-Functional Work Through Observation, Implementation, and Qualification

   Make it clear that collaboration is built into the model, not optional and that every team activity must include cross-functional participation.
2. Facilitate and Coach Early Collaborative Interactions

   Especially early on, use facilitators (project managers, team leads) to guide conversations, ensuring all voices are heard equally.
3. Distribute Leadership Opportunities Across Domains

   Rotate leadership of workshops, feedback sessions, and presentations among clinical, IT, and admin representatives to balance influence.
4. Measure and Celebrate Collaborative Success

   Recognize cross-functional teamwork explicitly, not just individual or departmental achievements.
5. Use Shared Language and Shared Goals

   Focus communication on shared patient care, operational excellence, and hospital mission goals, not only on technical milestones.

Further Reading

- *Team of Teams: New Rules of Engagement for a Complex World*, General Stanley McChrystal
- *Collaborating with the Enemy: How to Work with People You Don't Agree with or Like or Trust*, Adam Kahane

Rapid Learning and Evolution

Hospitals are learning environments; your HIS must be too. Organizational learning theory in healthcare and the concept of the *Learning Health System*, which emphasizes continuous knowledge generation and application within healthcare institutions[28].

Rapid Learning and Evolution refers to the continuous process of gaining insights, applying lessons immediately, and refining both the system and workflows as the project progresses.

It emphasizes speed, adaptability, and practical adjustment, rather than waiting until the end of a project to assess what went right or wrong.

In HIS implementations, Rapid Learning means:

- Capturing real-time feedback from users and stakeholders.
- Acting quickly on lessons learned after each cycle of development or deployment.
- Continuously evolving workflows, configurations, and training approaches based on new knowledge.

In essence, it's learning while doing, and evolving while delivering.

HIS touches everything from emergency care to pharmacy management to financial billing.

Because healthcare environments are dynamic and complex, static planning simply doesn't work well. Unexpected realities always emerge:

- Workflows that looked good on paper might fail under real clinical pressures.
- Regulatory changes might demand immediate system adjustments.
- New technologies or hospital strategies may arise mid-implementation.

Without rapid learning and evolution:

- Teams stick to outdated plans even when they clearly no longer fit.
- End-user frustration grows because their feedback is ignored or delayed.
- Operational risks increase when problems are discovered too late.

With strong rapid learning and evolution:

- System improvements are continuous, not episodic.
- Staff engagement rises as they see their feedback make an impact.
- The final system is finely tuned to real hospital needs, not assumptions.

How the Core Interaction Model (CIM) Supports Rapid Learning and Evolution:

It reinforces rapid learning and evolution through continuous Qualification (ongoing validation and improvement) and iterative cycles of development and observation.

Here's how:

Continuous Qualification

- CIM doesn't treat quality and validation as "end-of-project" events.
- Every cycle of implementation is paired with immediate Qualification activities: Testing, validating, and refining.
- This ensures real-time learning and constant improvement.

Iterative Cycles of Development and Validation

- Each increment of HIS development is observed, tested, improved, and validated before moving forward.
- Lessons learned from one module (example Admission) are immediately applied to the next (example Pharmacy).
- Feedback from real-world use is fed back into system design in the next cycle, not after full go-live.

By combining these two forces, CIM turns HIS implementation into a living, learning, and adapting process, instead of a rigid, pre-planned exercise.

Practical Tips for Fostering Rapid Learning and Evolution with CIM:

1. Hold Mini-Retrospectives After Each Increment

   After each feature/module rollout, run a quick review session: What worked? What didn't? What do we change for next time?
2. Use a Living Lessons-Learned Register

   Keep an active, easily accessible document or platform where all observations, lessons, and feedback are logged and visible to the entire project team.

3. Make Iterative Improvements Public
   Show users how feedback from earlier phases directly improved later modules. This builds trust and participation.
4. Embed Observers in Real Operations
   Place Observation team members inside daily workflows (example in wards, clinics) to capture early learning opportunities.
5. Design for Flexibility, Not Perfection
   Build workflows and configurations assuming they will need updates after real-world use, don't aim for "perfect on the first try".

Common Mistakes and Fears in Rapid Learning and Evolution

- Mistake: Waiting for Big Reviews Instead of Small Adjustments
  - Managers may fear that frequent evaluations create chaos, preferring big milestone reviews. Problems compound unnoticed until they become major crises.
- Mistake: Ignoring Early Feedback Because "It's Too Early to Judge"
  - Teams may believe initial user feedback isn't representative and dismiss it. Small problems grow into systemic issues.
- Mistake: Over-Planning for Perfection
  - Project leaders might think planning every detail perfectly up front is safer. Plans quickly become outdated, and adapting feels like failure rather than progress.
- Mistake: Collecting Feedback but Not Acting on It
  - Teams may collect feedback to "check the box" without having a real mechanism for applying it. User trust is damaged, and engagement drops.

How to Address These Mistakes and Fears with CIM

1. Normalize Iterative Validation Through Continuous Qualification
   Show that immediate testing and improvements are standard practice – not a sign of mistakes.
2. Use Observation-Driven Learning Cycles
   Structure short cycles where observations directly trigger adjustments, showing visible evolution.

Table 3.11 Rapid Learning and Evolution with CIM

Category	*Key Concepts/ Actions*	*Common Mistakes and Fears*	*CIM-Based Solutions and Practical Tips*
Continuous Qualification	- Validation and improvement occur continuously, not at the end - Each cycle includes testing, feedback, refinement	- Waiting for big milestone reviews - Fear that frequent evaluation disrupts progress	- Normalize real-time validation - Show that adjustments reflect maturity, not failure
Iterative Development Cycles	- Learn from each module and apply lessons immediately to the next - Observation, testing, and validation are built into every step	- Ignoring early feedback - Thinking "it's too early to judge" - Over-planning upfront	- Use mini-retrospectives after each rollout - Keep a living lessons-learned register - Build for flexibility, not perfection
Feedback Integration	- Feedback from real-world use directly informs next iteration - Continuous loop between system use and design	- Collecting feedback without applying it - Users lose trust when their input is ignored	- Publicly show how feedback influenced improvements - Use live dashboards or sprint reviews to connect insights to actions
Cultural and Team Mindset	- Embrace learning as part of progress, not a sign of failure - Celebrate early identification of improvement opportunities	- Seeing change as rework or failure - Leadership ignoring lessons learned	- Reward adaptation and flexibility - Keep leadership engaged in reviewing learning data - Embed observers in real operations to surface small issues early

3. Reward Teams for Early Detection and Adaptation
   Celebrate the identification of improvement opportunities, not just the final delivery.
4. Apply Lessons Immediately, Not Later
   Build mechanisms (like sprint reviews, live feedback dashboards) to quickly incorporate learnings into the next development phase.
5. Keep Leadership Actively Reviewing Learning Logs
   Ensure that hospital leadership reads rapid learning reports regularly, reinforcing the importance of adaptability from the top down.

Further Reading

- *The Lean Startup*, Eric Ries
- *Accelerate: The Science of Lean Software and DevOps*, Nicole Forsgren, Jez Humble, and Gene Kim
- *Learning to Improve: How America's Schools Can Get Better at Getting Better*, Anthony Bryk et al.
- *Scrum: The Art of Doing Twice the Work in Half the Time*, Jeff Sutherland
- *Dynamic Capabilities and Strategic Management*, David J. Teece

System Usability and User Empowerment

The success of any Hospital Information System (HIS) depends fundamentally on whether clinicians are able and willing to use it. Research demonstrating that clinician acceptance and sustained use are primary determinants of EHR success and impact[29]. No matter the size of the budget or the sophistication of the technology, a project will not succeed if the system is not adopted by its intended users.

System usability describes how easily and effectively users can interact with the HIS to accomplish their tasks. An effective system is intuitive, efficient, and closely aligned with established workflows. Such a system supports users in their daily responsibilities and avoids causing frustration or confusion.

User empowerment involves equipping users with the knowledge, confidence, and tools necessary to engage actively with the system. This includes the ability to customize certain features and to provide ongoing feedback for improvement. Empowered users are not merely operators; they are active contributors to the system's ongoing success. Participatory informatics and co-production models in digital health demonstrating user contribution to system refinement and sustainability[30].

In summary, a system that is easy to use enables users to perform their duties effectively. When users are empowered, they contribute positively to the system's development and performance. Conversely, even the most advanced technology will not succeed if it is difficult to use or if users feel they have no influence over its operation, regardless of the resources invested.

In hospital environments, where time is limited and mistakes can have serious consequences for patients, both usability and user empowerment are essential and cannot be compromised.

Without good usability and empowerment:

- Users resist or avoid the system, preferring manual workarounds.
- Errors and inefficiencies increase, endangering patient safety.
- Morale declines among staff, worsening change resistance.
- HIS ROI (Return on Investment) is never fully realized.

When usability and empowerment are prioritized:

- Staff use the system willingly and effectively.
- Continuous improvement becomes part of the culture.
- System adoption is faster, deeper, and more sustainable.
- Patient care and operational efficiency improve dramatically.

How the Core Interaction Model (CIM) Supports Usability and Empowerment

The Core Interaction Model (CIM) places Performance at the center of success metrics, not just completing deliverables and in CIM, Performance explicitly includes system usability and stakeholder satisfaction as core goals, not secondary afterthoughts.

Here's how:

Usability and Stakeholder Satisfaction as Core Performance Metrics in CIM

- Continuous Observation ensures that usability challenges are detected early during real-world operation, not after full system deployment.
- Dynamic Feedback Loops allow users to highlight usability pain points immediately, prompting fast improvements.
- Qualification activities include real-world validation of system usability – not just technical testing.
- Incremental Implementation allows users to adapt gradually, building confidence and empowering them to co-create better workflows.

Through these mechanisms, CIM builds usability and user empowerment into the system itself, instead of bolting them on at the end.

Practical Tips for Improving Usability and Empowering Users with CIM

1. Involve End Users Early and Continuously
   Engage real users during system design, configuration, and testing – not just at go-live.
2. Design for the "Average" and the "Edge" Cases
   Ensure workflows work not only for typical scenarios but also for exceptions and special cases users regularly encounter.
3. Offer Customization Options Where Appropriate
   Allow users (example physicians, nurses) to personalize views, templates, and workflows where flexibility improves efficiency without compromising standards.
4. Provide Practical, Role-Specific Training
   Focus training on real tasks users need to perform, not just system navigation.
5. Create Visible Channels for Ongoing User Feedback
   Make it easy and non-punitive for users to report usability issues or suggest improvements after go-live.

Common Mistakes and Fears in System Usability and User Empowerment

- Mistake: Designing for Management, Not End Users
  - Project teams may fear losing leadership buy-in if they prioritize usability over executive requests. Systems meet reporting needs but frustrate frontline workers, leading to underuse or resistance.
- Mistake: Assuming One-Size-Fits-All
  - IT and project leaders may fear that offering customization will complicate support. Users are forced into rigid workflows that don't match real-life needs, increasing dissatisfaction.
- Mistake: Limiting User Input to Pre-Go-Live Stages
  - Project teams may think user feedback post-go-live means failure in planning. Without ongoing input, usability issues persist and worsen.
- Mistake: Treating Training as a One-Time Event
  - Managers may fear that continuous training looks like bad planning, preferring one big rollout. Staff fall behind as the system evolves, and confidence erodes.

How to Address These Mistakes and Fears with CIM

1. Prioritize End-User Needs in Observation and Qualification
   Use Observation to monitor daily workflows and focus validation efforts on how well the system supports real tasks, not just technical functions.
2. Celebrate and Enable Flexibility Through Implementation
   Build options for personalization where possible while maintaining system standards, making users feel empowered rather than trapped.
3. Normalize Continuous Usability Feedback Loops
   Treat user feedback as essential performance data, not complaints, and highlight improvements made based on user suggestions.
4. Integrate Lifelong Learning into the HIS Strategy
   Recognize that training is a continuous need, especially as systems update, regulations change, and workflows evolve.
5. Measure Success in Terms of Stakeholder Satisfaction and Operational Efficiency
   Use KPIs that track user satisfaction scores, task completion times, and error rates alongside traditional project delivery metrics.

Table 3.12 Usability and Empowerment with CIM

Category	*Key Concepts / Actions*	*Common Mistakes and Fears*	*CIM-Based Solutions and Practical Tips*
Usability as a Core Metric	- Usability and stakeholder satisfaction are key performance indicators - Observations detect issues during real use - Qualification validates real-world usability	- Designing for management over frontline users - Fear of deprioritizing leadership needs	- Monitor daily workflows via Observation - Validate usability through Qualification - Prioritize system alignment with real user tasks
User Feedback and Adaptability	- Dynamic feedback loops allow users to report issues - Incremental implementation supports continuous improvement	- Limiting user input to pre-go-live phases - Seeing post-go-live feedback as failure	- Create easy, visible feedback channels - Highlight fixes driven by user suggestions - Normalize feedback as a tool for growth, not criticism
Empowerment Through Flexibility	- Offer personalization options where appropriate - Co-create workflows with users	- Assuming one-size-fits-all - Fear that customization increases support burden	- Allow role-specific customization without breaking system integrity - Celebrate adaptive solutions co-designed with users
Training and Learning	- Practical, task-based training - Lifelong learning integrated into HIS strategy	- Treating training as one-time event - Fear that ongoing training appears like poor planning	- Deliver role-specific, real-life scenario training - Update training as system and workflows evolve
Measurement of Success	- KPIs include user satisfaction, task efficiency, error rates	- Relying only on traditional project delivery metrics	- Use qualitative and quantitative usability KPIs - Include operational efficiency and stakeholder feedback in success definitions

Further Reading

- *Designing for Interaction: Creating Smart Applications and Clever Devices*, Dan Saffer
- *Don't Make Me Think: A Common Sense Approach to Web Usability*, Steve Krug
- *The Design of Everyday Things*, Don Norman
- *Usability Engineering*, Jakob Nielsen

Planning HIS Implementation

Implementing a Hospital Information System (HIS) involves more than technical deployment. It requires a comprehensive approach that integrates structured project management with the realities of hospital operations. Establishing clear and aligned project objectives at the outset is essential to ensure the HIS provides tangible clinical, administrative, and operational benefits.

An ongoing needs analysis is necessary to refine requirements as hospital conditions change. This process should be supported by careful resource allocation and risk management. Emphasizing system usability and empowering users are important steps to promote adoption and minimize resistance[31]. Incorporating dynamic feedback and iterative development cycles allows the system to adapt in line with stakeholder needs and evolving hospital workflows[3].

Effective data management and interoperability are critical for ensuring smooth information flow across departments and with external systems. Planning in this area must address data integrity, accessibility, and security. These measures help maintain reliable and secure access to information throughout the hospital.

Coordinating cross-functional teams requires clear communication and well-defined roles. Assigning responsibilities for observation, implementation, and qualification enables the project to benefit from specialized expertise. This structure supports efficient collaboration and project progress.

Successful HIS planning must remain adaptable. Valuing dynamic feedback, adopting iterative development practices, and encouraging ongoing stakeholder collaboration are necessary to maintain project resilience in a complex healthcare environment.

Cultural transformation should be recognized as a strategic priority. Achieving HIS success depends on shifting mindsets as well as implementing new technologies. Continuous engagement, empowerment, and trust-building activities should be integrated throughout the project lifecycle. The Core Interaction Model (CIM) supports these principles, ensuring that performance, usability, and stakeholder satisfaction are ongoing objectives pursued at every stage of the HIS implementation.

Successfully implementing a Hospital Information System (HIS) requires more than relying on standard project plans. It is important to recognize and address the specific challenges and characteristics of healthcare settings. The eight points outlined below offer a structured and practical approach, grounded in established project management principles and adapted to the unique demands of HIS implementation.

This guidance is relevant for project managers, clinical leaders, IT professionals, and executive sponsors alike. Careful consideration of these points will provide essential insights for aligning objectives, engaging stakeholders, managing risks, ensuring usability, and supporting sustainable cultural change. Reviewing each point thoroughly will help establish a strong foundation for effective and patient-centered HIS implementation planning.

1. Clear and Aligned Project Objectives

Hospital Information System (HIS), particularly electronic health records (EHRs), need to be assessed using specific success metrics. It is necessary to define real methods to increase efficiency and output. Conducting analysis requires a systematic development process to carefully evaluate each strength and weakness, based on work and business requirements. Health informatics evaluation methodologies recommending structured, multi-phase assessment models for system analysis[32]. This analysis can help prioritize objectives and allocate resources. According to Adams, the following elements are crucial for success[33]:

Project Objectives:

- Current workflows and processes.
- Alignment between project goals and current processes.
- System capabilities to cover operational gaps.
- Associated risks (technical and operational).

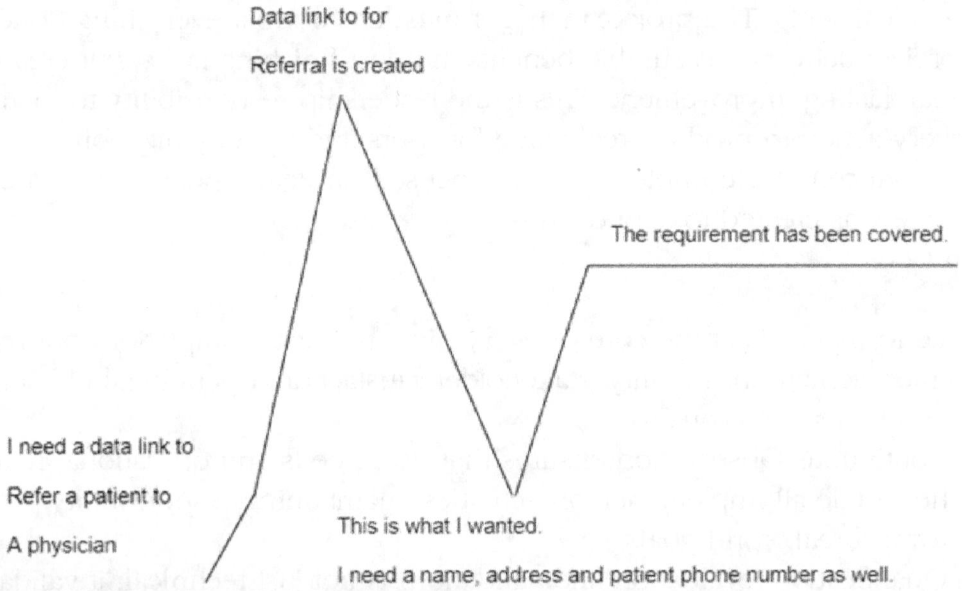

Figure 3.1 Diagram of a need or request[33]

Analyzing priorities helps organizations identify and allocate resources effectively, and prevent potential mistakes. Below are key risks:

- Failure to understand the needs of both sides of the project.
- Expansion of the project scope, gradual inclusion of unanticipated possibilities.
- Missing deadlines.
- Failing to meet project objectives.

Requests and demands always exist, meaning that even after implementation or decision-making, there may be requests for details or changes. The team responsible for developing the system might encounter revisions or redesigns, which will help with assessing needs for a better result at a lower cost in future revisions during the system's development stage.

- Key Point: Implementing a Hospital Information System (HIS), particularly with electronic health records (EHRs), will not fulfill the needs unless those needs are well-measured, prioritized, and sufficient resources and planning are allocated.

A project manager needs to responsibly protect the interests of all stakeholders and the broader environment of the project (example hospital, patients, and clinical staff). The project manager must ensure that everything done in the project delivers measurable benefits, not just finishing tasks, but creating real, lasting improvement. This is the leadership responsibility to focus on every action to produce real value for users and the organization. The "Performance-Centric Implementation Focused on Real Operational Value" principle was created to support this.

In CIM:

- Performance is at the core of everything, not just "completion" but real improvement in usability, stakeholder satisfaction, operational efficiency, and patient care quality.
- Continuous Observation ensures that user needs and operational realities guide all implementation activities, maintaining responsibility toward real-world goals.
- Qualification (evaluation and validation) is not just technical, it validates if real value (better processes, safer care, higher efficiency) is being delivered continuously.

Core Interaction Model (CIM):

- Protects operational integrity by constantly aligning system development with real hospital needs.
- Ensures stakeholder-centered value is created at every cycle through dynamic feedback, continuous adaptation, and usability-focused implementation.
- Guides resource use responsibly, focusing effort only where it truly improves healthcare operations, user satisfaction, and patient outcomes.

Healthcare Insight:

- HIS must deliver timely, accurate, usable data to clinicians, administrators, and patients.
- Objectives must align with actual workflows (clinical, administrative, and financial), not just theoretical goals.
- HIS success is measured not by software delivery alone, but by user satisfaction, operational efficiency, and patient care improvement.

Actions:

- Define user-centered objectives early.
- Align goals with current hospital processes, not force processes to fit the system.
- Focus on usability, efficiency, and stakeholder satisfaction as success indicators.

2. Needs Analysis and Continuous Requirements Discovery

For the analysis of needs, the analysis should be positive and precise. Both behavioral and life-cycle needs are important to simplify the need analysis process. When a deviation from the original course is detected, it must be reviewed again to prevent the organization from deviating from the desired process.

Requirements must be actively discovered, analyzed, validated, and updated throughout the project lifecycle. It's not just about gathering initial requirements once, it's about continuously uncovering evolving needs as the environment changes. Understanding and adapting to real user needs must happen continuously, not just during planning.

The CIM (Core Interaction Model) principle, "Observation-Driven Analysis and Real-Time Requirement Refinement", makes sure that:

- Observation is a continuous function, not a one-time activity.
- Observers are embedded in hospital operations and constantly gather insights from real user behavior, evolving workflows, and new operational demands.
- Dynamic feedback loops ensure that requirements are refined iteratively, not assumed to be static.

How CIM Reflects Needs Analysis:

- Captures emerging needs through daily Observation and stakeholder engagement.
- Continuously refines and reprioritizes requirements based on real-world operational feedback and evolving clinical needs.
- Minimizes mismatch between what is built and what is actually needed, enhancing system relevance and adoption.

Healthcare Insight:

- Conduct positive, precise needs assessments, covering behavioral, clinical, and life-cycle needs.
- HIS must evolve based on continuous feedback, because needs are dynamic, especially in healthcare.
- Failure to understand evolving needs leads to project failure, unmet objectives, and costly rework.

Actions:

- Implement structured, ongoing observation and feedback loops (not just at the start).
- Prioritize clinical usability, accessibility, and information flow needs.
- Allow flexible revision of requirements during implementation phases.

3. Resource and Risk Planning

Identifying, allocating, and managing resources (people, systems, time, and budget) and anticipating risks (technical, operational, and human) throughout the project, emphasizes proactive planning, risk mitigation, and efficient use of specialized skills to reduce uncertainty and improve delivery outcomes. It's about having the right people doing the right work and managing uncertainty with foresight and structure. The "Domain-Centered Role Assignment and Iterative Risk Mitigation" principle in CIM make sure:

- Resource planning is operationalized by assigning clearly defined roles to domain experts: Observation (needs analysts), Implementation (developers/configurators), and Qualification (validators/testers).
- This ensures that resources are aligned with their expertise and no critical domain is left unaddressed.
- Risk is managed iteratively, as Observation continuously monitors for issues and Qualification verifies alignment, enabling early identification and correction.

How CIM Reflects Resource and Risk Planning:

- Optimizes resource use through domain-specific role assignments, preventing overload and misalignment.

- Reduces risk exposure through continuous cycles of Observation and Qualification.
- Avoids scope drift and bottlenecks by embedding real-time issue detection and stakeholder-specific task ownership.

Healthcare Insight:

- Key risks: Scope creep, misunderstanding requirements, missing deadlines, and insufficient resource allocation.
- HIS planning must account for technical risks, operational disruptions, and user adaptation risks.
- Resource planning must ensure adequate skilled personnel (IT, clinical champions, and trainers).

Actions:

- Define a clear scope with mechanisms to manage change.
- Identify technical, operational, and behavioral risks early.
- Assign domain-specific roles (clinical, technical, and quality assurance) clearly from the start.

4. System Usability and User Empowerment

The HIS must be intuitive, efficient, and supportive of real user tasks, while empowering users to participate in improving and shaping it. A successful HIS is one that people want to use, because it helps, not hinders, their work. The "Performance-Driven Development with Usability and Stakeholder Satisfaction" principle in CIM, at its core, makes sure:

- Performance is not just about system uptime or delivery, it's measured by usability, workflow efficiency, and stakeholder satisfaction.
- The model prioritizes continuous Qualification, ensuring that user experience is evaluated not once, but repeatedly.
- Users are empowered through Observation, where their input directly influences design and adaptation.

How CIM Reflects System Usability and User Empowerment:

- Treats user satisfaction and ease of use as central to defining system performance.

- Enables users to be co-designers, not passive recipients, thanks to dynamic feedback loops.
- Provides continuous learning opportunities and allows users to guide incremental improvements.

Healthcare Insight:

- HIS must be attractive, easy to use, and efficient in real clinical environments.
- Staff must be empowered, trained, and actively involved in system design and feedback.

Actions:

- Embed usability testing into every stage of system development.
- Provide ongoing role-specific training and easy reporting mechanisms for system issues.
- Prioritize user empowerment through customization, quick support, and participation in decision-making.

5. Dynamic Feedback and Iterative Development

When is the implementation of a Hospital Information System (HIS) successful? In a real environment, the success rate of the Hospital Information System (HIS) implementation is determined by the interaction between senior managers and middle managers within the hospital. Organizational trust and leadership behavior influencing technology adoption and perceived legitimacy of systems[34]. As a result, trust in the system is also defined by this interaction. It is also likely that the system may be somewhat removed from the realities of the medical environment, and as a result, the project's outcome is influenced by external consultation from the organization. Only through this interaction with different success centers and through measuring various benchmarks can the system's success rate be evaluated. Multidimensional evaluation frameworks emphasizing benchmarking across financial, clinical, operational, and satisfaction indicators[35]. Economic factors play a significant role in determining why a project's budget exceeds expectations, as seen in cases where rapid access to information was a determinant of project success.

Consequently, the success metrics need to be set up according to pre-existing standards and immediately evaluated based on the feedback received from users, including staff satisfaction, user compliance, and quality of information provision. A hospital manager might perceive system success through different filters and expect different results from various experts, which can change how success is measured. Some may emphasize patient satisfaction, user adherence, and positive outcomes, while others might focus on whether the system has had any economic impact or changed care processes.

Success is dynamic, and hospital managers may have different priorities throughout the system's implementation and must adapt to changing expectations. It is also vital to measure the system's success after implementation, as standards and benchmarks may evolve. Continuous attention to standards and how user satisfaction with the system unfolds is crucial for long-term success[36].

NOTE:

Software changes are natural following the design of the system. They present the most significant challenge before and after installation, especially in managing these changes.

Changes in the software can arise when the system requires updates or improvement. These changes can generally be classified into three categories:

1. Minor changes: Changes that relate to specific details of the software interface or user operations.
2. Moderate changes: Changes that lead to improvements in system performance.
3. Major changes: Changes that lead to shifts in the primary goals and operations of the system.

The degree of success in implementing Hospital Information System (HIS) lies in the transition toward optimal system performance after installation and implementation. The best approach is to strengthen the health information management team, whose goal is to improve system efficiency. Typically, this team includes medical experts from both the clinical and health information management sides.

When changes in the system request more functionality after implementation, it's crucial that the team is ready to handle the challenges effectively. These challenges may include organizational adjustments or technical improvements to ensure long-term system success.

By involving experienced professionals, the team can anticipate difficulties and employ evidence-based strategies to improve system performance. Understanding both the human and technical factors is vital, ensuring that changes are managed efficiently, and that there is alignment with the overall goals of the healthcare center.

The key to success is continuous observation and adjusting the system's goals and requests to different sections of the healthcare facility.

Requests for system improvement must be prioritized to maximize organizational impact. The prioritization method, which categorizes and ranks requests, can include evaluation by a specialized committee. The review method involves classifying the various viewpoints in requests, such as clinical or financial requests. Primary evaluations are then followed by secondary evaluations based on the importance of the requests. Requests that have received more feedback or align with organizational priorities will be given more weight.

Here are important criteria that could be considered when prioritizing enhancements and changes in HIS:

Quality and Effectiveness

Scoring Criteria

- Improving clinical outcomes and enhancing treatment processes based on scientific evidence or improving communication with users.
- Increasing the quality and effectiveness of part of the project for success in subsequent projects.
- Increasing the quality and effectiveness of part of the project.

Efficiency and User Satisfaction

Scoring Criteria

1. Reducing the number of steps/time for a task.
2. Automating a manual process.
3. Reducing attention to risk.

Legal Considerations

Scoring Criteria

1. The organization is able to gather and present transparent data, ensuring security and confidentiality control, thus improving workflows.
2. It prepares the organization for upcoming institutional audits and legal inspections, with improvements expected within three months.
3. The organization improves its scientific reputation, being viewed as a reference by other medical centers.

Patient Safety

Scoring Criteria

1. Reduces the likelihood of data not being stored.
2. Increases the security of patient data.
3. Enhances patient safety during treatment.

Financial Issue

Scoring Criteria

1. It impacts the costs more than the agreed amount (above the agreed figure).
2. It impacts the costs up to the agreed amount (within the agreed figure).

Impact on Organizational Work/Level of Urgency

Scoring Criteria

1. It impacts more than 50% of data transfer within the organization.
2. It impacts less than 50% of data transfer within the organization.
3. A specialized team must follow up to manage the impact.

Exception

In cases where the request leads to a reduction in service disruption at the hospital, it is given higher priority.

The Hospital Information System (HIS) and electronic medical records can face issues due to structural, technical, or human shortcomings, making it temporarily unavailable. If these issues arise during system implementation, patient safety, continuity of care, and treatment services may be affected. Lack of access to the system might not only increase risks but also lead to medical errors or lack of access to patient records, which are critical for decision-making. Therefore, a crisis management plan must be in place for such situations, addressing system unavailability.

After the issue is resolved, the system must return to standard operation, with plans in place to ensure the workflow and organizational processes continue smoothly.

Also, the data that enters the system during a failure through unbacked-up databases must be managed. The use of mobile-based technology can assist with crisis management in real-time. After system implementation, decision-making must be done regarding whether all data can be stored electronically. In some cases, this might not be possible due to various reasons, including legal matters, forms, or paper-based records. For example, some data may need to be stored in paper format or in parallel systems. In certain situations, the data may need to be processed simultaneously through multiple systems, which will help ensure that the treatment process is followed accurately.

As systems become more integrated, the accumulation of system data grows daily. System failures require careful monitoring and awareness of the information flow, and any lack of attention could lead to significant problems in day-to-day healthcare center operations. These failures can result in a complete organizational breakdown, affecting the entire workforce, and causing disruptions in using and maintaining the system.

It should be considered that after the implementation and installation of the system, a complete evaluation must be conducted to determine if system management is effective. This process involves reviewing software lifecycle changes and ensuring that both technology advancements and organizational transformation are aligned. Questions may arise, such as: Was the system implementation successful, and were its challenges addressed? Was there proper user participation throughout the process? Was the timeline followed? Were user satisfaction and compliance met? Were the project's goals and standards achieved?

Analyzing the process during implementation and documenting these challenges helps prevent similar problems in future projects. This continuous review can ensure that lessons are learned from the system's weaknesses and strengths, aiding in future implementations.

Finally, don't forget to celebrate success. Celebrate your achievements at different stages of implementation with all the staff in the healthcare center or with patients.

Projects must learn and adapt in real time, not just follow a fixed plan. Teams should incorporate frequent feedback from users and stakeholders. Development must be incremental and responsive, refining the solution as conditions evolve.Projects should be learning systems, guided by feedback, evolving iteratively toward better outcomes.

Agility Through Iterative Development and Dynamic Feedback Loops principle in CIM, make sure:

- Observation feeds real-time insights into the implementation stream.
- Each cycle (Observation, Implementation, Qualification) allows for fast adaptation.
- Feedback is continuous and tightly integrated, not delayed until the end.

How CIM Reflects Dynamic Feedback and Iterative Development

- Encourages short feedback loops between users and implementers.
- Promotes incremental delivery, allowing course correction before major resources are wasted.
- Builds responsiveness into the model, enabling continuous evolution of both the system and the process.

Healthcare Insight:

- Change is inevitable (new clinical workflows, regulatory shifts, etc.).
- HIS must evolve through continuous feedback and incremental releases, not big-bang deployments.

Actions:

- Plan for continuous Observation, Implementation, and Qualification cycles (as emphasized in the Core Interaction Model).
- Run micro-iterations (example by module, department) with real-user testing and feedback incorporation.
- Accept and celebrate early adaptations rather than resisting them.

6. Data Management and Interoperability Planning

Data represents the repeatable presentation of information and knowledge in a formal method suitable for communication, interpretation, or processing by humans or machines. Information consists of data that is linked to a specific entity, truth, event, object, person, process, or concept. Knowledge consists of information.

In general, Healthcare information is about specific concepts within a particular domain (such as illness, treatment methods, etc.)

Health information refers to any kind of data communicated verbally or in written form that pertains to a person's health in any format.

Health information refers to data related to an individual's medical history, treatment plans, laboratory results, imaging, and clinical encounters, which is collected, stored, and shared by healthcare professionals and systems. Evidence-based health information is derived from validated clinical research, expert consensus, and patient data, ensuring that healthcare decisions are informed by the best available evidence.

According to the World Health Organization (WHO), health information includes "all the data and information produced by healthcare organizations and systems, used to deliver healthcare and track patient outcomes". It forms the basis for public health strategies, policy-making, and individual patient care.

Electronic Health Records (EHRs) are a prime example, enabling real-time access to a patient's medical history, thereby improving diagnosis, treatment, and patient safety. Systematic reviews demonstrating EHR contribution to information accessibility, coordination, and safety improvements[37]. Evidence also shows that access to comprehensive health information contributes to better health outcomes by facilitating data-driven decision-making in both individual and population health management.

Healthcare providers, when treating a patient, whether through a healthcare institution, a public organization, an insurance company, a school, or a university, or a service provider offering care in a home environment, create information based on their services.

This information relates to the patient's physical or mental condition in the past, present, or future. It is also related to a person's payment for healthcare services in the past, present, or future, which in turn influences the provision of health services to that person.

Health service providers maintain these healthcare data electronically and for several important reasons, including:

1. Improved Patient Care and Safety:
   The patient's medical record plays a key role in managing and planning their care. The patient's medical record is the primary reason for retaining medical documentation, as it ensures the patient's information is up to date for continued care. Healthcare managers rely on this documentation to ensure all medical considerations are met in the treatment process, while certain other purposes, like billing and payment, also depend on the medical record. Electronic Medical Records (EMRs) and Electronic Health Records (EHRs) improve patient care by providing clinicians with real-time access to accurate and up-to-date patient information. This reduces errors, ensures timely treatments, and facilitates better decision-making. A study published in the Journal of Patient Safety found that EHRs can reduce medication errors by up to 80%, as they provide automated alerts and check for potential adverse drug interactions.
2. Increased Efficiency and Productivity:
   Electronic health systems streamline administrative processes, reduce paperwork, and enable quicker access to patient information, allowing healthcare providers to spend more time on patient care. According to a report by Health Affairs, hospitals using EHRs experienced a 15% increase in productivity due to faster record retrieval and streamlined workflows, leading to shorter wait times for patients.
3. Enhanced Data Security:
   EHRs provide advanced security measures, such as encryption and access control, to safeguard sensitive patient information against unauthorized access and data breaches. A study published in *The Journal of Healthcare Information Management* demonstrated that healthcare organizations using EHRs experienced a 50% reduction in data breaches compared to those using paper-based records, thanks to more robust security features.
4. Cost Reduction:
   EHRs reduce costs associated with paperwork, storage, and manual processes, such as medical transcription and administrative staffing. They also reduce duplicative testing and improve billing accuracy. *The American Journal of Managed Care* found that healthcare providers using EHRs saw a 10-15% reduction in operational costs due to reduced paperwork, fewer duplicative tests, and more accurate billing processes.

5. Better Coordination of Care:
   EHRs facilitate seamless communication between healthcare providers, enabling better coordination of care, particularly for patients with complex or chronic conditions who see multiple providers. A study in *The New England Journal of Medicine* revealed that patients whose care was managed using EHRs experienced a 30% improvement in care coordination, leading to better outcomes and fewer hospital readmissions.
6. Improved Public Health Monitoring and Disease Surveillance:
   Electronic health data allows for better tracking of disease trends, supports early detection of outbreaks, and provides valuable data for public health research and policy-making. The Centers for Disease Control and Prevention (CDC) reported that EHR data significantly improved the speed and accuracy of public health surveillance during the COVID-19 pandemic, helping authorities make timely interventions.
7. Patient Empowerment and Engagement:
   EHRs give patients access to their own medical records, allowing them to take an active role in managing their health, schedule appointments, and communicate with healthcare providers. A Pew Research Center survey found that 64% of patients who accessed their health data through patient portals felt more empowered to manage their health conditions and better prepared for medical appointments.
8. Regulatory Compliance and Legal Requirements:
   EHRs ensure that healthcare providers meet regulatory requirements, such as HIPAA in the US, by maintaining detailed audit trails and securely storing medical records. A study published in *Health IT and Policy* showed that 90% of healthcare organizations using EHRs reported full compliance with national regulatory standards, significantly reducing their risk of legal penalties.
9. Communication:
   Medical records are essential tools for communication between healthcare providers, doctors, nurses, and other caregivers. They facilitate communication about the patient, especially for long-term care. Medical records allow staff to communicate efficiently about a patient's care during hospitalization, treatment periods, or after years of interaction with the patient.
10. Research and Quality Management:
    Medical records are always used as sources for research and to evaluate the quality of care provided. They can serve as a detailed reference

to assess the delivery of care, providing a foundation for further studies. Universities, research institutions, and healthcare providers rely on this data to analyze and improve future treatment methods. Many studies utilize patient records for research on best practices in improving patient care. Researchers may be encouraged to study patient outcomes without the cost of patient care, taking advantage of the technology and learning from the results. Without data and information, healthcare systems are not required. Health information is a valuable asset for health organizations, and other sectors rely on it. Healthcare administrators need to ensure that the correct information about the resources and data related to healthcare is used.

Healthcare is evolving rapidly, and the use of computer-based tools in healthcare is increasing. New technologies such as mobile devices, bedside tools and Artificial Intelligence will multiply the expansion of these technologies. Hospital networks now have educational systems based on computers to improve the learning capabilities of healthcare professionals. Administrators are making efforts to create integrated documentation systems for effective learning and better management. For instance, tools based on computer learning, such as electronic health records, can improve health and treatment globally. This includes support for specialists and cooperation with healthcare professionals to provide access to reliable information at all levels.

An information system can be defined as a socio-technical system in which an organization can process information. This includes all the factors involved in data processing, such as technical factors or human-related elements. In the social aspect of an information system, the interactions among people and their data are considered. In healthcare, this means that the tools used by people to process information must be capable of handling medical tasks. The steps necessary to create such a system are based on healthcare professionals' guidelines, which are applied via information technology. Support systems for communication, like electronic health records, include the resources needed for proper information management. Another important system is a Hospital Information System (HIS), which contains several tools for processing social and technical information relevant to patients and staff. This system ensures that the organization's data is properly processed and managed efficiently.

NOTE:

Information systems in healthcare centers are not necessarily computer-based, and in these centers, in addition to technical aspects, they also have social dimensions.

Data Creation: Problems related to how data is created are likely to be more important than other issues. The key aspects related to data creation are listed below but are not limited to these points:

- Timely Access:
  During medical procedures, different users may need access to certain data. The system must be designed to provide access to the following items at the right time:
- Basic data for the patient's medical record.
- Cumulative data received from a group of patients.
- Dynamic data received from various databases.
- Database Compatibility:
  This means whether the data stored in one database can be transferred to another, or whether the database system supports data communication.
- Dynamic Linking:
  Dynamic links must be created to ensure the transfer of data either within or outside the organization when necessary.
- Skill Requirements:
  One of the challenges of using IT in hospitals is creating and using data in the hospital's information system. IT skills must be fostered among hospital staff.

Data Management: The way data is managed relates to architecture, workflows, and policies regarding how data is created and maintained over time. The key aspects of data management are listed below but are not limited to these points:

Key aspects of data management include, but are not limited to:

- Data Accessibility: Ensuring that authorized personnel can access the necessary data when required, while maintaining confidentiality and security protocols.

- Data Integrity: Maintaining the accuracy and consistency of data throughout its lifecycle to prevent errors and unauthorized alterations.
- Data Storage and Backup: Implementing reliable storage solutions and regular backup procedures to safeguard against data loss.
- Data Security: Protecting data from unauthorized access, breaches, and other security threats through robust security measures.
- Compliance with Standards: Adhering to legal and regulatory requirements for data management, including patient privacy laws and industry standards.

Data Utilization:

How data is used within the organization affects decision-making, patient care, and operational efficiency. The key aspects of data utilization include, but are not limited to:

- Decision Support: Leveraging data analytics to inform clinical and administrative decisions, improving patient outcomes and organizational effectiveness.
- Training and Education: Providing staff with the necessary training to effectively use data systems and understand data-related policies.
- Process Improvement: Using data to identify areas for improvement within workflows and processes, enhancing overall efficiency.
- Knowledge Sharing: Facilitating the sharing of data and insights among departments to promote collaboration and unified patient care.
- Performance Monitoring: Utilizing data to monitor performance metrics, ensuring that organizational goals are being met and identifying opportunities for growth. A set of distributed databases that use intelligent modules for their orchestration and information management.

Key issues related to data sharing are not limited to the following points:

- Data Interoperability:

  The ability to link and exchange data between distributed databases, enabling a Hospital Information System (HIS) to effectively share data. This is achieved through a mechanism that supports data exchange between different database systems.

- Data Accessibility:
  A network platform that facilitates secure data exchange, encryption, and transfer of data packages. It should also ensure that communication protocols are updated for effective access.
- Information and Communication Technologies:
  This term refers to a broad range of technologies used for data sharing in healthcare, including standards like HL7 or tools like email.
- Multiple Data Formats:
  All types of data formats should have the potential for sharing.

Data Display:

Data collected from distributed systems can be aggregated and displayed in different formats. Different user interfaces might be required to display such data. Critical issues related to data presentation are not limited to the following points:

- Dynamic Format:
  Can these types of data be displayed with limitations on the client-side?
- Widespread browser compatibility:
  All types of browsers in a web environment should be supported by the Hospital Information System (HIS), backed by CSS formatting.
- Ease of Use:
  The system's ease of use in displaying data for various therapeutic objectives should be acceptable.
- How is data displayed in a treatment center via a Hospital Information System (HIS), with a wide range of data accepted and seamlessly integrated? Will the response to the display request be smooth and timely?

Data must be accurate, accessible, secure, and consistently managed throughout the system's lifecycle. HIS system must be designed with interoperability in mind, meaning smooth data exchange between internal modules and external healthcare systems. Proper planning for data flow, integrity, security, and connectivity is critical to healthcare quality and operational success.Good data governance and seamless data sharing are foundational to an effective HIS.

Integrated Operations with Focus on Data Integrity, Accessibility, and Interoperability principle in CIM make sure:

- Observation and Implementation are fully connected to real hospital operations, including workflows around data creation, sharing, and storage.
- Interoperability challenges are caught early during Observation and addressed iteratively.
- Qualification activities validate not only usability but also data accuracy, integration, and accessibility across systems.

How CIM Reflects Data Management and Interoperability Planning

- Treats data flow and interoperability as part of ongoing operational Observation, not just as technical specs.
- Ensures that data usage, quality, and security are evaluated dynamically throughout system evolution.
- Focuses on real operational integration, meaning HIS is not a separate island, it functions as part of the larger healthcare ecosystem.

Healthcare Insight:

- HIS must handle data creation, management, storage, interoperability, and display reliably and securely.
- Without proper data architecture, the hospital will face operational chaos.

Actions:

- Design robust data governance frameworks early (covering security, privacy, backup, data sharing).
- Ensure interoperability standards (example HL7, FHIR) are embedded in technical designs.
- Plan dynamic data linking across departments and external facilities for continuity of care.

7. Communication and Role Management

In the current state of care, the healthcare of patients involves many different individuals, and often there is a need for the collective sharing of patient data among all involved. Care coordination and continuity literature emphasizing multidisciplinary involvement and shared patient information[38]. This calls for the integration of complex communication across various healthcare and medical systems . Health information exchange (HIE) research highlights cross-system integration as essential for coordinated care[39]. The complexity and intricacy of communications within health systems increase the likelihood of errors and risks during the exchange of results and interpretations of medical data. The use of such data requires cautious handling of patient care and other services.

The medical field requires significant data sharing across various levels of the health system to maintain quality standards of care. For healthcare providers, it is crucial to exchange health data related to a patient's care with other organizations, nearby hospitals, or centers involved in the patient's care journey. Additionally, producing or using health information must be continuously exchanged across the various processes and services required for patient treatment . Healthcare services that involve continuous care and monitoring, especially in patient information sharing, are needed across all healthcare facilities for quality improvement.

Interoperability standards and frameworks (e.g., FHIR-based exchange models) supporting seamless internal and external data sharing[40]. Hospital Information System (HIS) must adopt a model where data is efficiently exchanged and shared, providing a continuous connection within the system and externally between healthcare facilities .

Health and medical communication must follow a standard flow that connects healthcare professionals, institutions, insurance, and other relevant parties in an organized manner. Health communication and structured data exchange standards emphasizing standardized workflows and messaging protocols[41]. Each step of the process must involve the accurate and timely transmission of the required data . Miscommunication between healthcare professionals can lead to disruptions in continuity of care, with the potential to harm patient satisfaction and delay necessary treatment.

In short, effective and timely data transfer is critical in ensuring the satisfaction of patients, the confidence of physicians, and the optimal use of healthcare resources.

The health system's communication involves multiple approaches and layers, ensuring access to a diverse audience. Information sharing related to health, for policy-making, guidance, advocacy, and community involvement, allows stakeholders, especially decision-makers, to make informed decisions and improve outcomes. Public health informatics literature demonstrating the role of health data in policy development and decision-making[42].

Systems designed for easing communication must consider the necessary foundational structures, especially for hospital staff who play different roles. For instance, in a hospital, a nurse or doctor may fulfill different roles depending on the time, the shift, or even the condition of a patient. A cardiologist, for instance, plays a significant role in the hospital's emergency department during cardiac emergencies but could have a different role entirely in the cardiology department on regular shifts.

One major challenge in designing Hospital Information System (HIS) is ensuring that they facilitate communication between caregivers and researchers.

1. Patients: Health records, supported by software capabilities, can manage patient data, while researchers, through management protocols, oversee how this data is used for research purposes.
2. Caregivers: It is crucial that those involved in providing care have complete access to patient information, especially when data is also required by researchers. However, researchers may have restricted access depending on the case.
3. Hierarchy Issues: A major communication gap exists between caregivers and researchers because of their different positions within healthcare organizations.

The Crucial Difference Between Negotiation and Communication in Project Success:

In my experience, negotiation and communication play distinct yet equally crucial roles in the success of any project. Negotiation is often what gets a project off the ground, setting the terms and conditions that guide its course. However, it's communication that drives the project forward, ensuring it reaches completion.

Negotiation focuses on establishing agreements, but communication is the key for understanding, collaboration, and creativity. It enables the project team to navigate challenges and develop solutions effectively. Without strong communication skills, even the most specialized teams will struggle, often facing financial difficulties and unnecessary disputes over invoices and project terms.

In the context of implementing a Hospital Information System (HIS) in a complex, multidisciplinary environment like a hospital, effective communication is what keeps all stakeholders motivated and aligned. A lack of communication, on the other hand, can undo years of effort and turn a promising system into a legacy burden. Many HIS projects have failed not due to technical issues but because communication broke down along the way.

If you ever find yourself in a situation where project discussions have devolved into arguments over contract terms and threats of non-payment, it's a clear sign that communication has faltered. Remember, it's not negotiation but consistent, positive

Clear, structured, and consistent communication between all stakeholders throughout the project is very important. Proper role definition and management, ensuring every participant knows their responsibilities, authority, and contribution to project success. Facilitating effective collaboration and reducing misunderstandings. Strong communication and clear role ownership are vital for aligned, efficient, and resilient project execution.

Unified, Cross-Functional Team Collaboration with Clear Domain-Centered Roles principle in CIM, make sure:

- Teams are intentionally cross-functional, clinical, administrative, IT, and quality specialists work together, not separately.
- Roles are domain-centered: Observation, Implementation, and Qualification responsibilities are assigned clearly based on expertise.
- Communication is continuous between these functions through dynamic feedback loops, not siloed or hierarchical.

How CIM Reflects Communication and Role Management

- Establishes natural communication channels through cross-functional team structures.
- Clarifies responsibilities early by tying tasks to Observation, Implementation, or Qualification activities.
- Encourages real-time feedback and collaboration among different professional groups, promoting transparency and agility.

Healthcare Insight:

- Communication must be role-sensitive (different needs for doctors, nurses, IT, administration, and researchers).

- HIS must facilitate clear, timely, and secure communication across the hospital and with external partners.

Actions:

- Map communication flows carefully for both technical teams and operational staff.
- Build cross-functional, collaborative teams with clear Observational, Implementation, and Qualification responsibilities.
- Train users in both technical use and data-sharing protocols.

8. Cultural Transformation Planning

Successful project outcomes often require shifts in organizational mindset, behaviors, and culture, not just installing a new system or process[3]. Cultural change must be planned, nurtured, and continuously reinforced to achieve lasting adoption. Staff must be prepared, engaged, supported, and empowered to embrace the new way of working. You don't just change systems, you change mindsets, habits, and working cultures.

Cultural Transformation Embedded Through Continuous Stakeholder Engagement, Feedback Loops, and Collaboration principle in CIM, make sure:

- Cultural adaptation isn't treated as a separate side-task, it is naturally built into the core mechanics of the model.
- Through continuous Observation, dynamic feedback, and cross-functional collaboration, users are engaged early, heard continuously, and empowered to participate in system evolution.
- This repeated interaction shifts mindsets gradually, building trust, ownership, and confidence in the change.

How CIM Reflects Cultural Transformation Planning

- Ensures early and ongoing engagement, embedding new behaviors over time.
- Creates a feedback-driven environment where users see real impact from their contributions.

Healthcare Insight:

- HIS implementation is as much a cultural change as a technical project.
- Staff must move from "paper-centric" or "department-centric" mindsets to system-centric, data-driven, and collaborative workflows.

Actions:

- Engage early influencers and clinical champions to drive acceptance.
- Communicate vision and benefits continuously, not just at kickoff.
- Integrate change management activities throughout the project (training, forums, and recognition programs).

Further Reading

- RFP sample documents as tools for use by healthcare organizations: Online from: https://aem-prod.oklahoma.gov/content/dam/ok/en/okhca/documents/a0500/15024.pdf
- Winter A, Haux R, Ammenwerth E, Brigl B, Hellrung N, Jahn F. *Health Information Systems: Architectures and Strategies.* London: Springer Science & Business Media; 2011.
- Soriano FI. *Conducting Needs Assessments: A Multidisciplinary Approach.* Thousand Oaks (CA): SAGE Publications; 2012.
- Daigrepont J. *Complete Guide and Toolkit to Successful EHR Adoption.* Chicago (IL): HIMSS; 2011. p. 129–134.
- Paton RA, McCalman J. *Change Management: A Guide to Effective Implementation.* 3rd ed. London: SAGE Publications; 2008.
- Lee C, Robinson L, et al. The preparedness of hospital health information services for system failures due to internal disasters. *Health Information Management Journal.* 2009;38(2):18–26.
- Socio-technical system. In: Encyclopedia.com [Internet]. Available from: http://www.encyclopedia.com/social-sciences/dictionaries-thesauruses-pictures-and-press-releases/socio-technical-system
- Haux R, et al. *Strategic Information Management in Hospitals: An Introduction to Hospital Information Systems.* New York (NY): Springer; 2004. p. 25–26.
- Haux R, et al. *Strategic Information Management in Hospitals: An Introduction to Hospital Information Systems.* New York (NY): Springer; 2004. p. 27–28.

- Wager KA, et al. *Health Care Information Systems: A Practical Approach for Health Care Management.* 2nd ed. San Francisco (CA): Jossey-Bass/ John Wiley & Sons; 2009. p. 89–104.
- Glossary of Health Information Technology Terms: Available from: http://www.chirocare.com/wp-content/uploads/2013/03/HITTerms.pdf
- Wilson P, McEvoy S. *HealthIT Jump Start.* Indianapolis (IN): John Wiley & Sons; 2012. p. 15–16.
- Lu X, Zhang H, et al. The architecture of enterprise hospital information systems. In: *Proceedings of the 27th Annual International Conference of the IEEE Engineering in Medicine and Biology Society*; 2005; Shanghai, China. p. 6071–6074.

System Evaluation and Selection

Paper records and traditional written documentation are no longer sufficient to address the demands of today's advanced healthcare sector. Research documenting limitations of paper-based systems and the need for digital records to support complexity, safety, and scalability[43]. With the emergence of the Hospital Information System (HIS) and other technological advancements, reliance on outdated methods has significantly diminished. Modern information systems now play a central role in facilitating communication, managing patient records, and ensuring the continuity of care within healthcare facilities. When selecting an appropriate Hospital Information System (HIS), it is essential to carefully evaluate all potential risks and specific requirements. Health IT procurement and evaluation literature emphasizing structured risk assessment before adoption[44].

The integration of information technology in healthcare offers several advantages, including:

- Reducing medical errors, such as those related to medication or diagnosis.
- Supporting healthcare professionals in delivering effective treatment.
- Enhancing access to up-to-date patient information.
- Improving the efficiency and quality of care.

Although the implementation of these systems involves considerable costs, the potential benefits are substantial. However, failures or shortcomings in information systems can negatively impact healthcare outcomes. For this reason, comprehensive evaluations are necessary to support informed decision-making by both managers and end users. Establishing clear and accurate assessment criteria is vital for identifying issues and confirming the effectiveness of a system throughout its lifecycle.

Initial studies should focus on the feasibility and cost-effectiveness of implementing a new system. Following deployment, further assessments are required to measure the system's effectiveness and overall performance. Systematic evaluations help determine whether the system meets its intended objectives, such as enhancing patient care.

Ultimately, the primary goal of any healthcare information technology system is not only to support clinical services but also to promote effective collaboration and communication among healthcare staff. Evaluation criteria should reflect how well the system aligns with the broader objectives of healthcare delivery, while also safeguarding the underlying information technology infrastructure.

NOTE:

Evaluation should accompany the entire lifecycle of information technology during the project.

Effective evaluation is essential for understanding the operational context of a Hospital Information System (HIS) and for determining whether the system is both safe and effective. Through evaluation, it becomes possible to identify any gaps within existing processes and to obtain results that are meaningful for stakeholders.

By defining evaluation in this manner, attention is directed toward analyzing and clarifying the key characteristics of the Hospital Information System (HIS), specifically in relation to its planning, design, development, and implementation. The primary objective is to generate outcomes that support informed decision-making within the hospital setting.

Evaluation should not only focus on the information system but also include organizational changes that the system introduces. In reality, the initial approach to evaluation involves understanding the changes brought about by the system. Sligo[45] points out the importance of evaluating Hospital Information System (HIS) by examining how they respond to the needs of the hospital. Vassilios[46] identifies multiple objectives for evaluation, including:

1. Measuring how well the system architecture matches the needs of the hospital.
2. Avoiding negative impacts on treatment processes.
3. Adapting to changes in the internal structure of the hospital.

Research on system evaluation can be either technical (focused on technological improvements) or managerial (focused on how development teams or system implementers improve the system's performance). The evaluation process raises many questions aimed at directing the information system toward achieving multiple goals, such as:

- Which technology should be selected and implemented?
- What are the technical and system features that will ensure better performance?
- Will the users adopt the technology and integrate it into their daily tasks?
- How proposed technology impacts organizational structure and the quality of processes (such as time-saving in patient admission or clinical tasks). Taking into account the various needs of different users like doctors, nurses, etc.
- The effects of information technology on the quality of care within the healthcare center.
- Will the proposed technology satisfy the hospital's needs?

The evaluation of a Hospital Information System (HIS) architecture is a critical process that extends from the initial design phase through to implementation. Careful analysis of the system's structure and its individual components is essential to ensure that the architecture supports overall quality.

The primary objective is to determine whether the system's architecture upholds the required standards for care processes, patient safety, and security. This assessment is particularly important, as these factors directly affect the effectiveness and reliability of healthcare delivery.

Evaluating the quality of a hospital system requires a thorough understanding of how the architecture aligns with established health and safety standards. In the early stages of design, specialists focus on whether the system's architecture meets both their expectations and regulatory requirements. It is important to note that variations in system features, even within the same architectural framework, can result in differing quality assessments.

Ultimately, the quality of a Hospital Information System (HIS) is largely determined by its software architecture. This architecture must not only address the needs of users but also comply with recognized software engineering standards to ensure a reliable and effective system.

Here are some methods of analyzing and evaluating system architecture[47]:

- SAAM (Software Architecture Analysis Method)
- QAW (Quality Attribute Workshop)
- ADD (Attribute-Driven Design)
- ATAM (Architecture Tradeoff Analysis Method)
- CBAM (Cost-Benefit Analysis Method)

Some specialists argue that evaluating information technology systems is complex because healthcare systems often involve a wide range of information. This complexity leads to various evaluation challenges, as the impact of information technology on patient care is not always clear.

Three main challenges exist in evaluating information technology in the healthcare industry, as follows:

- Separation of Evaluation Goals:

  When evaluating a part of an information system in an organization, one must consider a complete image, not just focused on the software and hardware. Instead, it should concentrate on the interaction between users and information technology. Therefore, the evaluation needs to assess not only the hardware and software but also how users interact with the system and the processes it facilitates.

Overcoming these Challenges:

- Technical Environment: The environment where the information technology is being implemented must be well-described, including not only the software and hardware used but also the experiences of the users and their engagement with the system. Motivation for the system's adoption is crucial to measure, as is the introduction of new technical capabilities for implementing the system. Any new legal or compliance issues must be clearly outlined.
- Continuous Evaluation: Evaluation is an ongoing process that doesn't just end when the system is selected. Real-time evaluations throughout the system's life cycle ensure that any required modifications are made. Multiple stages of evaluation must be carried out, and at each step, the system's readiness for implementation must be assessed.
- System Success: Evaluation must measure the success of the system in achieving the specific goals defined at the outset. For example, whether

the system reduces the length of patient stays or improves overall patient care.

- Project Evaluation Challenges: Complex healthcare environments with diverse users pursuing different goals make it challenging to measure the system's success. Some users aim to make information storage and retrieval easier, while others focus on improving decision-making processes. All of these goals must be aligned and evaluated continuously to ensure that the system is functioning well.

Proposed solutions for managing this challenge:

- Preparing an evaluation plan should be the first step.
- Evaluation should consider the available resources and tools.
- Adequate time must be allocated for designing the evaluation process.
- All quantitative and qualitative elements that need to be measured must be considered carefully.
- To answer every question during evaluation, an appropriate method must be selected.

Motivation for Evaluation:

Evaluation is only feasible when sufficient financial and human resources are available to complete the process. Often, motivation at the senior management level in healthcare facilities plays a key role. Sometimes, high motivation arises out of fear of receiving negative feedback from an evaluation or not having enough time for staff training.

Solutions for managing this challenge:

- Increasing the number of human resources involved in the evaluation process with a combined approach. First, the organization's senior managers must be motivated to participate in the evaluation process. Second, motivation should be created through incentives, such as training staff in relevant technologies, which can encourage long-term engagement in the evaluation process.
- Financial incentives for hiring additional human resources can help create motivation. This should be coordinated across different departments by the evaluation team.

Recommendations for overcoming challenges related to Hospital Information System (HIS) evaluation:

1. Evaluation should be conducted systematically, considering the impact of the Hospital Information System (HIS) across all departments.
2. Evaluation must be based on the organization's goals and perspectives in relation to the Hospital Information System (HIS).
3. Since implementation often involves unpredictable changes, the evaluation must also observe the effects of these changes.
4. Evaluation must include the differences between design, production, and real implementation conditions in the actual environment.
5. The gap between users and the responsibilities they hold regarding information technology must be measured.
6. Involving users is important when evaluating system participation in the implementation process.

Information technology plays a significant role in healthcare centers, particularly in environments where increasing virus resistance is a concern. The application of advanced IT solutions has become essential for enhancing the quality and efficiency of healthcare services.

Modern technological devices now feature highly complex systems that can be designed with relative ease. The integration of robust software and hardware, along with advanced network security measures, is introducing new perspectives and raising expectations within the healthcare sector.

Investing in information technology has become a critical process for hospitals. Studies linking IT investment to organizational performance and digital maturity in hospitals[48]. Hospital administrators are increasingly faced with the challenges associated with integrating health information technology into these multifaceted environments.

Hospital Information System (HIS) serve a broader purpose than simply managing daily reporting and data transfer. They are instrumental in supporting decision-making processes at all organizational levels, particularly in the creation and management of information. Clinical decision support and health informatics governance literature identifying HIS as a foundation for managerial and clinical decision-making[49].

The selection of hospital software, especially electronic health records, is a complex and long-term commitment. Expectations and requirements may evolve over time, presenting ongoing challenges if not anticipated in advance. Furthermore, organizational needs can differ based on the unique culture of each hospital.

- It is essential to carefully evaluate the capabilities of any software under consideration.
- Attention should be given to the availability of necessary updates and ongoing support.
- The choice of software vendor is a critical decision, as unresolved issues in the commercial relationship may have adverse effects.

Selecting an appropriate information system is a critical undertaking that involves three distinct phases: Prior to implementation, during implementation, and following implementation. Each phase requires careful planning and attention to detail to ensure the success of the project.

The process of selecting an information system typically involves several key steps:

- Defining the project's objectives and primary mission
- Conducting a thorough needs analysis
- Preparing a request for information
- Developing a request for proposals
- Engaging in negotiations
- Drafting contractual agreements
- Establishing the system implementation team
- Transferring responsibilities to the selected implementation team

It is important to recognize that time constraints can arise during the system selection process. In such cases, the selection team must remain mindful of the available timeframe and be prepared to address potential challenges. Understanding the reasons behind the duration of the selection process is essential for effective planning.

Additionally, the responsibilities of the system selection team include negotiating terms and determining costs and pricing. These considerations must be integrated into the overall project execution. Insufficient time allocated to the selection process may negatively impact system implementation, potentially resulting in project delays or reduced performance by the implementation team.

The relationship between information systems and organizational strategy is of significant importance. Strategic alignment theory linking IT systems to organizational objectives and competitive advantage[50]. Implementing an information system is a key factor in achieving organizational goals and executing strategic plans. For organizations that prioritize investment, aligning the chosen information system with strategic objectives is essential.

In environments such as hospitals, it is particularly important for the selected system to support efficient operations within a clinical setting. The system must possess the necessary capabilities to adapt to the specific requirements of the healthcare environment.

Stage 1: Identifying needs and goals

To ensure that the selected information system meets the organization's goals and clearly defines its expectations, the system selection process begins with the information technology team and clinical staff. Two important expectations from the Hospital Information System (HIS) are financial and clinical treatment goals.

Stage 2: Formulating the organization's strategy

Once the goals and expectations of the system have been clearly defined, the executive team should establish five key strategies for success. These include human resource development, patient safety, and aligning resources with governmental standards.

Stage 3: Consideration of information systems

Executives, managers, and clinical staff must ensure that the selected system meets the organization's needs and goals, aligns with the hospital's strategy, and creates strong cooperation between the clinical team and the system. At this stage, teamwork is highly crucial because they can prioritize the organization's needs and identify the key factors to consider for the system.

Gathering data from vendors, reviewing the centers where the final system has been installed, and talking with the users of that system will help to make decisions in consideration.

Members of the team who collaborate in understanding information technology can benefit more by encouraging the use of ideas and measuring needs. This process helps in selecting and assessing suitable ideas from among the existing needs and proposals.

Stage 4: Information System Approval

The final review of the selected information system by managers, IT specialists, and clinical staff is necessary for ensuring successful implementation and making sure that it aligns with the organization's strategy. The confirmation of the information system throughout the evaluation process includes the degree of investment return, experience, and analysis of its functionality. Observing how the information system operates in hospitals can encourage more acceptance among clinical staff.

Stage 5: Implementation

Project managers, in collaboration with the final system users, approve the system and begin installing it on a trial basis. This step offers an initial opportunity for user training and continued implementation to maximize the system's potential for success in achieving goals and aligning with the organization's strategy.

NOTE:

In the healthcare and treatment sector, it has been mentioned that there are challenges in the software selection process and that many reports focus on the specific need to choose appropriate software. The same is true for the team responsibility, as the selected software may differ significantly from what is expected.

Establishing the primary objectives, timeline, and budget of a project is closely linked to the planning phase. During the software selection stage, it is essential to maintain consistency in the project's main goals. Significant changes to these objectives can adversely affect both the project's progress and its schedule. An inadequate selection process may also compromise the achievement of goals, disrupt the timeline, and lead to budget overruns.

This principle extends to the roles of managers and clinical staff. Any misalignment between the chosen system and the actual needs of these stakeholders can result in substantial challenges. Altering project objectives after the initial planning phase will likely have a negative effect on both the timeline and the overall implementation.

Selecting Hospital Information System (HIS), particularly electronic health records (EHRs), involves several challenges. A key consideration is ensuring that the chosen system supports the effective design and deployment of information systems within healthcare facilities. The EHR solution itself must be capable of addressing these requirements.

While it is advisable to pursue the development of such systems, caution is necessary when evaluating software providers, even those offering highly regarded products. The same level of scrutiny should be applied when selecting vendors for system production or when assembling teams for clinical centers, as these decisions significantly influence the project's success.

In the context of health information technology, open-source solutions can be particularly valuable in certain situations. Recent trends indicate that many software vendors are adopting open-source approaches and are prepared to offer support when required. As a result, vendors are increasingly demonstrating their capabilities not only in software development but also in providing ongoing support, especially when they can maintain consistent service delivery.

It is therefore important for vendors to implement effective support strategies and to ensure that their client base is sufficiently robust. The quality and reliability of the services provided are critical factors in supporting healthcare organizations.

Vendor Requirements

- Vendors should allocate a portion of their annual budget to research, system development, and independent support services.
- Each company must maintain an independent office and have an active presence in the city where the healthcare center operates.

Key Considerations for Hospital Information System (HIS) Implementation

- Vendor Presence at Medical Centers:

  It is essential for the vendor of the Hospital Information System (HIS), particularly the electronic health record (EHR), to be physically present during system installation and operation. On-site reviews help identify hidden costs, enhance user satisfaction, and provide insight into how the company addresses issues during implementation.
- System Trial:

  Request that the vendor conduct a system trial within the actual operational environment for a defined period. This trial should include full access to installation and a specified setup, allowing users to evaluate the system's strengths and weaknesses effectively.
- Contract Drafting:

  Careful drafting of contract terms and conditions is critical, with particular attention to sensitive points that could jeopardize the project.

Table 3.13 How CIM Supports HIS Evaluation and Selection

Category	*Key Concepts/ Actions*	*Common Mistakes and Fears*	*CIM-Based Solutions and Practical Tips*
Strategic Alignment	Align HIS with hospital's strategic goals, including financial and clinical outcomes	Misalignment between HIS features and hospital vision, ignoring stakeholder priorities	Use Observation phase to gather strategy-aligned requirements; conduct early stakeholder workshops
User Engagement and Adoption	Ensure users will adopt and use the system in daily tasks	Assuming users will adopt the system post-implementation, neglecting early input	Use Dynamic Feedback Loops; involve users in system trials and requirement validation
Feasibility and Cost-Effectiveness	Assess technical, financial, and operational feasibility before selection	Relying solely on vendor promises, ignoring operational constraints	Use Qualification to run pilots and compare projected vs. actual performance
Vendor and Architecture Evaluation	Evaluate vendor capabilities, architecture quality, and support readiness	Overlooking long-term vendor support; underestimating architectural complexity	Use architectural analysis methods (example ATAM, CBAM) in Observation; validate vendor support on-site
Lifecycle-Based Evaluation	Evaluate the system across the full project lifecycle	Focusing only on pre-implementation; no ongoing monitoring or feedback	Embed evaluation into Observation, Implementation, and Qualification phases continuously

(*Continued*)

Table 3.13 (Continued) How CIM Supports HIS Evaluation and Selection

Category	*Key Concepts/ Actions*	*Common Mistakes and Fears*	*CIM-Based Solutions and Practical Tips*
Organizational Impact	Understand how the system transforms workflows and responsibilities	Ignoring cultural and structural impacts; resistance to change	Map processes during Observation; monitor behavior and workflow shifts post-go-live
Uncertainty and Change Management	Account for changes in scope, goals, or regulations	Rigid plans unable to adapt to evolving needs; fear of rework	Keep implementation flexible; requalify system if significant changes occur
Evaluation Challenges	Balance diverse stakeholder expectations and complex evaluation tasks	Unclear evaluation metrics; difficulty aligning goals across departments	Define shared performance indicators and use real-time dashboards to monitor progress
System Trial and Real-World Testing	Test the system in actual operational environments before full deployment	Skipping trials; relying on demonstrations or references only	Use incremental implementation for hands-on testing with live feedback capture
Contracting and Vendor Relations	Draft robust contracts ensuring vendor accountability and long-term support	Vague SLAs; lack of consequences for vendor underperformance	Tie payment milestones to performance KPIs; require local vendor presence and active support

These terms should be thoroughly reviewed to support the project's success.

- Knowledge Management:
  Maintain up-to-date knowledge of project management practices by consulting scientific resources and databases regularly. This approach ensures that your understanding remains current and relevant.
- System Selection:
  It is not always necessary to install a new system if comparable alternatives from other providers meet your requirements. Carefully consider all available options before making a final decision.
- System Selection Process:
  Initiate the system selection process early, before resources such as time and other assets become constrained. Early planning helps ensure a smoother and more effective implementation.

How Core Interaction Model (CIM) offers advantages when applied to the Evaluation and Selection of Hospital Information System (HIS):

Further Reading

- Formative and Summative Evaluation: Online from: https://pcmh.ahrq.gov/sites/default/files/attachments/FormativeEvaluation_032513comp.pdf
- Example Evaluation Model and Its Review:
- De Morais RM, Somera SC, Goes WM, Costa AL. Applicability of an assessment model for healthcare information systems in a public hospital. *J Inf Syst Technol Manag.* 2016;13(3):459–478.
- Methods to Assess the Safety of Health Information Systems:
- Borycki E, Keay E. Methods to assess the safety of health information systems. *Healthc Q.* 2010;13:47–52.
- SAAM (Software Architecture Analysis Method):
- Kazman R, Abowd GD, Bass L, Webb M. SAAM: a method for analyzing the properties of software architectures. In: *Proceedings of the 16th International Conference on Software Engineering*; 1994 May 16–21; Sorrento, Italy. Los Alamitos (CA): IEEE Computer Society Press; 1994. p. 81–90.
- QAW (Quality Attribute Workshop):
- Barbacci M, Ellison R, Lattanze A, Stafford J, Weinstock C, Wood W. *Quality Attribute Workshops (QAWs)*, 3rd ed. Pittsburgh (PA): Software Engineering Institute, Carnegie Mellon University; 2003.

- ADD (Attribute-Driven Design):
- Clements P, Kazman R, Klein M. *Evaluating Software Architectures: Methods and Case Studies*. Boston (MA): Addison-Wesley Professional; 2002.
- ATAM (Architecture Tradeoff Analysis Method):
- Kazman R, Barbacci M, Klein M, Carriere S. Experience with performing architecture tradeoff analysis. In: *Proceedings of the 21st International Conference on Software Engineering*; 1999 May; Los Angeles (CA). p. 54–67.
- CBAM (Cost-Benefit Analysis Method):
- Kazman R, Asundi J, Klein M. Quantifying the costs and benefits of architectural decisions. In: *Proceedings of the 23rd International Conference on Software Engineering (ICSE '01)*; 2001 May; Toronto, ON, Canada. p. 297–306.
- Three mistakes that people make when selecting a new software system can be found at: https://www.bnncpa.com/resources/library/three_mistakes_people_make_when_selecting_a_new_software_system
- 15 important decisions in the temporary selection of an Electronic Medical Record (EMR) system:
- Gasch A, Gasch B. *Successfully Choosing Your EMR: 15 Crucial Decisions*. Chichester (UK): John Wiley & Sons; 2010.

Building a HIS Center of Excellence (CoE)

Many healthcare organizations are adopting a Center of Excellence (CoE) model to effectively govern and enhance their Hospital Information System (HIS). Digital governance and IT capability maturity literature describing Centers of Excellence as structures for enterprise-wide IT optimization and governance[51]. A HIS CoE serves as a centralized, multidisciplinary team responsible for defining and enforcing best practices, standardizing system usage, ensuring comprehensive training, and promoting innovation throughout the organization. This team functions as the strategic core for HIS governance and performance optimization, ensuring that system capabilities are aligned with clinical, administrative, and regulatory objectives.

Implementing a HIS CoE is crucial for hospitals aiming to maximize the value, consistency, and impact of their digital systems. As HIS environments become increasingly complex with various modules, user groups, and compliance requirements, decentralized management can result in workflow inconsistencies, duplicated efforts, and limited system adoption. A centralized CoE structure addresses these challenges by standardizing practices, overseeing system changes, coordinating training, and supporting ongoing improvement. Data governance maturity literature linking centralized governance to improved data quality and reliability[52]. This approach facilitates better alignment between clinical needs and technical solutions, maintains consistent data quality, and encourages the adoption of new digital tools. Ultimately, a HIS CoE contributes to greater efficiency, safety, and strategic use of health information technology across the organization.

Key Steps in Developing a HIS Center of Excellence

Establishing a HIS CoE involves several essential steps:

- Team Formation: Assemble a multidisciplinary team with representatives from IT, clinical informatics, data governance, operations, compliance, and project management.
- Governance Frameworks: Develop and implement governance structures, such as change control processes and data ownership policies.
- Standardization: Create standardized workflows and templates to ensure consistency across the organization.
- Training Coordination: Organize system training and onboarding programs to support effective system use.
- Evaluation and Improvement: Assess new features or modules to enhance efficiency and care quality.
- Monitoring and Feedback: Track user feedback, system adoption metrics, and incident reports to inform system enhancements and support decision-making.

By centralizing HIS leadership through a CoE, hospitals can reduce variation, improve data integrity, encourage cross-functional collaboration, and foster a culture of continuous learning and digital innovation.

How to Build a HIS CoE: Step-by-Step

1. Define the Mission and Scope

Start by clearly outlining the CoE's purpose. Is it focused on HIS optimization, support and training, innovation, or all of the above? Define scope areas such as:

- Governance and policy development
- Workflow standardization

- User training and competency
- Analytics and reporting
- System upgrades and innovation testing

2. Assemble a Multidisciplinary Team

Include representatives from:

- Clinical departments (example: physicians, nurses, and pharmacists)
- Health informatics
- IT and infrastructure
- Data governance
- Quality and compliance
- Training and education
- Project management

The team may have core members (permanent) and extended members (departmental liaisons).

3. Establish Governance Processes

Develop clear processes for:

- Change request evaluation and approval
- System customization and configuration standards
- Policy enforcement (example: naming conventions, data entry protocols)
- Data access control and privacy

This ensures that HIS changes are strategic, safe, and consistent.

4. Develop Training and Adoption Programs

Design centralized training for:

- New employees (onboarding)
- Super-users and clinical champions
- Advanced users (example: analytics, reporting tools)

Offer regular refresher courses and e-learning materials to sustain engagement and skill levels.

Table 3.14 How CIM Support in Building a HIS Center of Excellence (CoE)

Category	*Key Concepts / Actions*	*Common Mistakes and Fears*	*CIM-Based Solutions and Practical Tips*
Mission and Scope Definition	Define CoE purpose (optimization, training, and innovation) and scope (governance, workflows, and reporting)	Lack of clear focus; attempting to do too much at once	Use CIM Observation phase to gather needs across departments; define iterative, prioritized goals based on real operational challenges
Multidisciplinary Team Assembly	Include clinical, IT, governance, compliance, training, and project management representatives	Siloed teams with poor communication; missing key stakeholders	Leverage CIM cross-functional stakeholder loops to build aligned, performance-focused teams
Governance and Standardization	Set up change control, configuration standards, policy enforcement, and data governance	Chaotic change requests; inconsistent system usage; unclear policies	Apply CIM Qualification cycle to test and validate governance changes before full enforcement
Training and User Adoption	Centralize onboarding, super-user programs, and continuous training	Fragmented training; low engagement; over-reliance on vendor sessions	Use Dynamic Feedback Loops to track adoption challenges; update training based on real-time user experience
Performance Monitoring and Feedback	Track usage metrics, helpdesk reports, and user satisfaction for continuous improvement	Collecting data without acting on it; feedback fatigue among users	CIM's cyclic Observation and Qualification enable real-time data to inform decisions and targeted improvements

(*Continued*)

Table 3.14 (Continued) How CIM Support in Building a HIS Center of Excellence (CoE)

Category	*Key Concepts / Actions*	*Common Mistakes and Fears*	*CIM-Based Solutions and Practical Tips*
Innovation and Pilot Testing	Pilot emerging technologies (example AI, mobile apps), evaluate impact, and scale successful tools	Innovation trials that fail to scale or don't align with clinical needs	Use CIM Incremental Implementation to run small pilots, gather feedback, and iterate before full rollout
Executive Sponsorship and Alignment	Secure leadership support and ensure CoE aligns with hospital strategy	Weak authority; limited resources; misalignment with executive goals	Observation phase includes strategic mapping to gain leadership buy-in and resource commitment
Scalability and Adaptability	Ensure CoE can evolve with new tech and organizational maturity	Rigid structures that resist change; fear of continuous restructuring	CIMs adaptive framework allows the CoE to grow with the hospitals digital maturity

5. *Monitor Performance and Feedback*

Track:

- System utilization metrics
- User satisfaction surveys
- Help desk issues and incident reports
- Audit logs and downtime statistics

Use this data for continuous improvement, targeted interventions, and decision support.

6. *Foster Innovation*

Empower the CoE to pilot new features or technologies (example AI tools, voice recognition, and mobile applications), evaluate their performance, and recommend system enhancements. This builds a culture of digital innovation within the hospital.

A Hospital Information System (HIS) Center of Excellence (CoE) provides a range of strategic and operational benefits that strengthen a hospital's digital health infrastructure. By centralizing governance, the CoE promotes consistent use of HIS tools, standardizes workflows, and enforces data entry protocols. This approach leads to enhanced data quality and greater system reliability.

The CoE also streamlines change management and training activities, which helps reduce implementation risks and supports faster user adoption. Clinicians benefit from digital tools that are better aligned with their workflows, while administrators gain improved oversight of system performance and compliance. Furthermore, the CoE offers a structured environment for evaluating and adopting new technologies, such as artificial intelligence solutions or mobile health applications. Collectively, these benefits contribute to increased clinical efficiency, improved patient safety, and a stronger long-term return on digital health investments.

The effectiveness and sustainability of a Hospital Information System (HIS) Center of Excellence depend on several critical factors. Strong executive sponsorship is necessary to provide the CoE with the required authority, visibility, and resources. Cross-functional collaboration is equally important, as it brings together clinical, technical, administrative, and informatics teams to ensure that decisions are practical and aligned with organizational objectives.

Clear governance structures and well-defined communication channels help streamline decision-making, reduce confusion, and support consistent adherence to standards across the hospital. Ongoing user engagement, particularly involving clinicians in testing, feedback, and improvement initiatives, fosters trust and encourages system adoption. Finally, the CoE must remain adaptable and scalable to keep pace with technological advancements and the hospital's evolving digital maturity. Together, these elements enable the CoE to standardize processes, drive innovation, and lead the HIS strategy effectively.

Further Reading

- Carter JH. *Electronic Medical Records: A Guide for Clinicians and Administrators.* Philadelphia (PA): ACP Press; 2001. p. 19–29.
- Carter JH. *Electronic Medical Records: A Guide for Clinicians and Administrators.* Philadelphia (PA): ACP Press; 2001. p. 30–41.

- Palmer M, Walters M. *Guide to Operating Systems.* Boston (MA): Cengage Learning; 2012.
- Rasmussen J, Zunde P, editors. *Empirical Foundations of Information and Software Science III.* Berlin: Springer Science & Business Media; 2012.
- Westbrook J, Callen J, editors. *Information Technology in HealthCare 2007: Proceedings of the 3rd International Conference on Information Technology in HealthCare: Socio-Technical Approaches.* Amsterdam: IOS Press; 2007.
- Elmasri R, Navathe SB. *Fundamentals of Database Systems.* 6th ed. Boston (MA): Addison-Wesley; 2011.
- Benson T. *Principles of Health Interoperability: HL7 and SNOMED.* London: Springer; 2010. p. 55–74.
- Winter A, Haux R, Ammenwerth E, Brigl B, Hellrung N, Jahn F. *Health Information Systems: Architectures and Strategies.* London: Springer Science & Business Media; 2011. p. 75–199.

References

1. Tsai CH, Eghdam A, Davoody N, Wright G, Flowerday S, Koch S. Effects of electronic health record implementation and barriers to adoption and use: A scoping review and qualitative analysis of the content. *Life (Basel).* 2020;10(12):327. doi:10.3390/life10120327.
2. Wesley DB, Schubel L, Hsiao CJ, et al. A socio-technical systems approach to the use of health IT for patient reported outcomes: Patient and healthcare provider perspectives. *J Biomed Inform.* 2019;100(Suppl):100048. doi:10.1016/j.yjbinx.2019.100048.
3. Project Management Institute. *A Guide to the Project Management Body of Knowledge (PMBOK® Guide).* 7th ed. Project Management Institute; 2021.
4. Cresswell KM, Sheikh A. Organizational issues in the implementation and adoption of health information technology innovations: An interpretative review. *Int J Med Inform.* 2013;82(5):e73–e86. doi:10.1016/j.ijmedinf.2012.10.007.
5. Alzghaibi H, Hutchings HA. The impact of leadership and management on the implementation of electronic health record systems in primary healthcare centers. *Healthcare (Basel).* 2024;12(20):2013. doi:10.3390/healthcare12202013.
6. Holden RJ, Karsh BT. The technology acceptance model: Its past and its future in healthcare. *J Biomed Inform.* 2010;43(1):159–172. doi:10.1016/j.jbi.2009.07.002.
7. Singh H, Sittig DF. Measuring and improving patient safety through health information technology: The health IT safety framework. *BMJ Qual Saf.* 2016;25(4):226–232. doi:10.1136/bmjqs-2015-004486.

8. McAlearney AS, Hefner JL, Sieck CJ, et al. Facilitating ambulatory electronic health record system implementation: Evidence from a qualitative study. *Biomed Res Int.* 2015;2015:629574. doi:10.1155/2013/629574.
9. Larman C, Basili VR. Iterative and incremental development: A brief history. *Computer.* 2003;36(6):47–56. doi:10.1109/MC.2003.1204375.
10. Lindgren R, Eriksson O, Lyytinen K. Managing identity tensions during mobile ecosystem innovation. *MIS Q.* 2015;39(2):359–384. (Agile/iterative and user co-creation principles applied in complex IT
11. Dingsøyr T, Nerur S, Balijepally V, Moe NB. A decade of agile methodologies: Towards explaining agile software development. *J Syst Softw.* 2012;85(6):1213–1221. doi:10.1016/j.jss.2012.02.033.
12. Sittig DF, Singh H. A new sociotechnical model for studying health information technology in complex adaptive healthcare systems. *Qual Saf HealthCare.* 2010;19(Suppl 3):I68-I74. doi:10.1136/qshc.2010.042085.
13. Ratwani RM, Reider J, Singh H. A decade of health information technology usability challenges and the path forward. *JAMA.* 2019;321(8):743–744. doi:10.1001/jama.2019.0161.
14. DeLone WH, McLean ER. The DeLone and McLean model of information systems success: A ten-year update. *J Manag Inf Syst.* 2003;19(4):9–30. doi:10.1080/07421222.2003.11045748.
15. Ammenwerth E, Iller C, Mahler C. IT-adoption and the interaction of task, technology and individuals: A fit framework and a case study. *BMC Med Inform Decis Mak.* 2006;6:3. doi:10.1186/1472-6947-6-3.
16. Bowens FM, Frye PA, Jones WA. Health information technology: Integration of clinical workflow into meaningful use of electronic health records. *Perspect Health Inf Manag.* 2010 Oct 1;7(Fall):1d.
17. Farzandipur M, Rangraz Jeddi F, Azimi E. Factors affecting successful implementation of hospital information systems. *Acta Inform Med.* 2016;24(1):51–55. doi:10.5455/aim.2016.24.51-55.
18. West MA, Lyubovnikova J, Eckert R, Denis JL. Collective leadership for cultures of high quality healthcare. *J Organ Behav.* 2014;35(2):240–260. doi:10.1002/job.1889.
19. Edmondson AC. Psychological safety and learning behavior in work teams. *Adm Sci Q.* 1999;44(2):350–383. doi:10.2307/2666999.
20. Lorenzi NM, Riley RT. Organizational issues = change. *Int J Med Inform.* 2000;69(2–3):197–203. https://doi.org/10.1016/S1386-5056(02)00105-3.
21. Keesara S, Jonas A, Schulman K. Covid-19 and healthcare's digital revolution. *N Engl J Med.* 2020;382(23):E82. doi:10.1056/NEJMp2005835.
22. Hill GM, Wang J. The project resilience framework: Building resilience in project organizations. *Int J Manag Proj Bus.* 2018;11(4):921–938. doi:10.1108/IJMPB-09-2017-0104.
23. Wears RL, Hollnagel E, Braithwaite J. Resilient healthcare: Turning patient safety on its head. *Int J Qual HealthCare.* 2015;27(5):418–420. doi:10.1093/intqhc/mzv063.

24. Wiig S, Aase K, Billett S, et al. Defining the boundaries and operational concepts of resilience in the healthcare literature. *BMC Health Serv Res.* 2020;20:330. doi:10.1186/s12913-020-05224-3.
25. Salas E, Reyes DL, McDaniel SH. The science of teamwork: Progress, reflections, and the road ahead. *Am Psychol.* 2018;73(4):593–600. doi:10.1037/amp0000334.
26. Reeves S, Pelone F, Harrison R, Goldman J, Zwarenstein M. Interprofessional collaboration to improve professional practice and healthcare outcomes. *Cochrane Database Syst Rev.* 2017;6(6):CD000072. doi:10.1002/14651858.CD000072.pub3.
27. Bate P, Robert G. Experience-based design: From redesigning the system around the patient to co-designing services with the patient. *Qual Saf HealthCare.* 2006;15(5):307–310. doi:10.1136/qshc.2005.016527.
28. Friedman CP, Allee NJ, Delaney BC, et al. The science of learning health systems: Foundations for a new journal. *Learn Health Syst.* 2017;1(1):e10020. doi:10.1002/lrh2.10020.
29. Gagnon MP, Desmartis M, Labrecque M, et al. Systematic review of factors influencing the adoption of information and communication technologies by healthcare professionals. *J Med Syst.* 2012;36(1):241–277. doi:10.1007/s10916-010-9473-4.
30. Carman KL, Dardess P, Maurer M, et al. Patient and family engagement: A framework for understanding the elements and developing interventions and policies. *Health Aff (Millwood).* 2013;32(2):223–231. doi:10.1377/hlthaff.2012.1133
31. Venkatesh V, Morris MG, Davis GB, Davis FD. User acceptance of information technology: Toward a unified view. *MIS Q.* 2003;27(3):425–478. doi:10.2307/30036540.
32. Kaplan B, Harris-Salamone KD. Health IT success and failure: Recommendations from literature and an AMIA workshop. *J Am Med Inform Assoc.* 2009;16(3):291–299. doi:10.1197/jamia.M2997
33. Adams WG. *Project Management for Healthcare Information Technology.* McGraw-Hill; 2005.
34. Weiner BJ. A theory of organizational readiness for change. *Implement Sci.* 2009;4:67. doi:10.1186/1748-5908-4-67.
35. Ash JS, Berg M, Coiera E. Some unintended consequences of information technology in healthcare: The nature of patient care information system-related errors. *J Am Med Inform Assoc.* 2004;11(2):104–112. doi:10.1197/jamia.M1471
36. Nilsen P. Making sense of implementation theories, models and frameworks. *Implement Sci.* 2015;10:53. doi:10.1186/s13012-015-0242-0.
37. Campanella P, Lovato E, Marone C, et al. The impact of electronic health records on healthcare quality: A systematic review and meta-analysis. *Eur J Public Health.* 2016;26(1):60–64. doi:10.1093/eurpub/ckv122.
38. Haggerty JL, Reid RJ, Freeman GK, Starfield BH, Adair CE, McKendry R. Continuity of care: A multidisciplinary review. *BMJ.* 2003;327(7425):1219–1221. doi:10.1136/bmj.327.7425.1219

39. Vest JR, Gamm LD. Health information exchange: Persistent challenges and new strategies. *J Am Med Inform Assoc.* 2010;17(3):288–294. doi:10.1136/jamia.2010.003673
40. Mandel JC, Kreda DA, Mandl KD, Kohane IS, Ramoni RB. SMART on FHIR: A standards-based, interoperable apps platform for electronic health records. *J Am Med Inform Assoc.* 2016;23(5):899–908. doi:10.1093/jamia/ocv189
41. Benson T, Grieve G. *Principles of Health Interoperability: SNOMED CT, HL7 and FHIR.* 3rd ed. Springer; 2016.
42. Yasnoff WA, Overhage JM, Humphreys BL, LaVenture M. A national agenda for public health informatics. *J Public Health Manag Pract.* 2001;7(6):1–9.
43. Chaudhry B, Wang J, Wu S, et al. Systematic review: Impact of health information technology on quality, efficiency, and costs of medical care. *Ann Intern Med.* 2006;144(10):742–752. doi:10.7326/0003-4819-144-10-200605160-00125
44. Boonstra A, Broekhuis M. Barriers to the acceptance of electronic medical records by physicians from systematic review to taxonomy and interventions. *BMC Health Serv Res.* 2010 Aug 6;10:231. doi:10.1186/1472-6963-10-231
45. Sligo J, Gauld R, Roberts V, Villa L. A literature review for large-scale health information system project planning, implementation and evaluation. *Int J Med Inform.* 2017;97:86–97. doi:10.1016/j.ijmedinf.2016.09.007
46. Aggelidis VP, Chatzoglou PD. Hospital information systems: Measuring end user computing satisfaction (EUCS). *J Biomed Inform.* 2012;45(3):566–579. doi:10.1016/j.jbi.2012.02.009
47. Bass L, Clements P, Kazman R. *Software Architecture in Practice.* 3rd ed. Addison-Wesley; 2013.
48. Menachemi N, Collum TH. Benefits and drawbacks of electronic health record systems. *Risk Manag Healthc Policy.* 2011;4:47–55. doi:10.2147/RMHP.S12985
49. Kawamoto K, Houlihan CA, Balas EA, Lobach DF. Improving clinical practice using clinical decision support systems: A systematic review of trials to identify features critical to success. *BMJ.* 2005;330(7494):765. doi:10.1136/bmj.38398.500764.8F
50. Chan YE, Reich BH. IT alignment: What have we learned? *J Inf Technol.* 2007;22(4):297–315. doi:10.1057/palgrave.jit.2000109.
51. Weill P, Ross JW. *IT Governance: How Top Performers Manage IT Decision Rights for Superior Results.* Harvard Business School Press; 2004.
52. Otto B. Organizing data governance: Findings from the telecommunications industry and consequences for large service providers. *Commun Assoc Inf Syst.* 2011;29(3):45–66.

Chapter 4

HIS Project Success in Smart Future Healthcare Ecosystem

Finally, we reframe HIS project management in smart hospitals. The Core Interaction Model (CIM) sits at the center, weaving stakeholder collaboration, adaptive governance, and real-time performance monitoring into a living framework. With CIM, HIS projects evolve into enduring, value-generating ecosystems instead of finite tech fixes.

In the emerging landscape of data-driven smart healthcare, the significance of a Hospital Information System (HIS) extends well beyond its initial deployment or routine operations. Although careful planning, effective execution, and ongoing management are fundamental to establishing a reliable system, the long-term strategic value of an HIS is determined by the manner in which health information is governed, protected, and utilized over time.

The healthcare sector is transitioning from environments where digital systems primarily facilitate data exchange among various sub-systems within a hospital to a new era characterized by cognitively connected hospitals. In this advanced setting, information systems do not merely support operational needs but play a central role in enabling informed decision-making and fostering continuous improvement (where systems think, decide, and act collaboratively).

NOTE:

Connected to the cognizant healthcare ecosystem is the next stage of digital health maturity.

DOI: 10.4324/9781003795254-4

Omid Rajaei defines a smart hospital as "A smart hospital is a digital hospital that uses smart technologies to create new capabilities and improve processes". In their systematic review of the literature (and industrial sources), Rajaei and colleagues analyzed 17 studies and identified 83 characteristics of smart hospitals, ultimately defining the concept in terms of technologies, services, and goals[1]. The Rajaei definition tends to be technology-centric and process-centric, capturing the diversity of "smart" features found across both academic and industrial literature.

Anastasia Levina defines smart hospitals as "Smart hospitals are institutions that optimize, redesign or build new clinical processes, management systems, and infrastructure in order to improve medical and economic performance by means of the latest technologies (in healthcare, management, IT)". This definition broadens the view: A "smart hospital" is not simply about using advanced devices, but about fundamentally rethinking processes, management, and infrastructure, leveraging a "smart infrastructure" (integrated networks of digital and physical assets) to deliver better services. The Levina definition takes a more holistic, systems-oriented view, highlighting that becoming "smart" involves redesigning not just technology but also processes, management, and infrastructure[2].

In considering the evolution of hospital digital transformation, it is important to recognize that the definition of a truly smart hospital in 2025 and beyond extends beyond the mere integration of devices and third-party systems. The hallmark of a smart hospital will not be the quantity of digitally connected systems, but rather the manner in which these tools interact intelligently.

Establishing a connected system remains a fundamental principle for achieving both data and digital maturity. While this connectivity represents an essential step toward digital transformation, it is only the foundation. Smart hospitals advance beyond simple connectivity; they function as cognizant systems where intelligence encompasses not only technical capabilities but also organizational alignment and the empowerment of staff. In these environments, hospitals continuously learn from their operations, leveraging context-aware tools to enhance performance.

Within a smart hospital, data moves seamlessly into an interoperable Hospital Information System (HIS) and advanced technological layers. These systems do more than report issues; they are designed to sense, interpret, and act ethically. As a result, the smart hospital becomes a dynamic and adaptive node within the broader healthcare ecosystem, connected, responsive, and aligned with human purpose.

Current vs. Future Smart Hospitals

- Current smart hospitals are characterized by digital connectivity and automation, utilizing integrated IT systems. Their primary objectives include improving operational efficiency, enhancing patient safety, and facilitating data integration.
- Future smart hospitals will function as adaptive, agentic health nodes. These institutions will be self-learning and autonomous, with systems that are continuously aligned with human purpose. The core objective will shift toward enabling ongoing, context-aware, and ethically autonomous care within an intelligent ecosystem.

The Evolving Role of Technology

- In current smart hospitals, technology primarily serves to collect data through Electronic Medical Records (EMR) and a Hospital Information System (HIS), and to share insights via analytics.
- In future smart hospitals, technology will take on a more advanced role, sensing, reasoning, and acting. This will be achieved by implementing sophisticated technology layers, such as artificial intelligence, which will coordinate and learn across various operational domains.

NOTE:

Technologies evolve rapidly. Information is accurate at the time of writing. Readers should verify current regulations and vendor capabilities.

Shift in Meaning – moving from record keeping to intelligent ecosystems

Historical analyses of medical record evolution demonstrate that the development of medical records closely reflects the broader progress of medicine. Initially, documentation was primarily used for educational and reference purposes, often relying on narrative accounts. Over time, patient records became formalized as integral elements of hospital operations, directly associated with quality, accountability, and the continuity of care[3].

As the concept of continuity of care gained prominence, it became evident that a transition was necessary from paper-based records to computer-assisted processes. This shift required the adoption of new tools, frameworks, and standards to support more efficient management of patient information.

In the decades that followed, electronic health records became widely implemented. Interoperability standards such as HL7 V2, HL7 V3, and FHIR were introduced, while policy initiatives further accelerated the digitization and exchange of healthcare data[4].

Currently, the healthcare sector is characterized by a stage of digital maturity. Hospital information systems (HISs) are evolving beyond static data repositories, and the process of digitization continues to advance.

Looking ahead, the field is moving toward the development of intelligent ecosystems. In the coming years, healthcare networks are expected to become increasingly dynamic, leveraging artificial intelligence to support real-time learning, prediction, and decision-making (Figure 4.1).

It is essential to recognize the reasons why many hospitals encounter difficulties in progressing from being merely connected to becoming truly cognizant. The challenges involved are not limited to technical issues; they also encompass organizational, cultural, and strategic factors[5].

As the healthcare sector advances toward intelligent Hospital Information System (HIS) ecosystems, several persistent obstacles continue to arise, many of which extend well beyond the realm of technology. Numerous hospitals operate with fragmented system architectures. Although technical integration

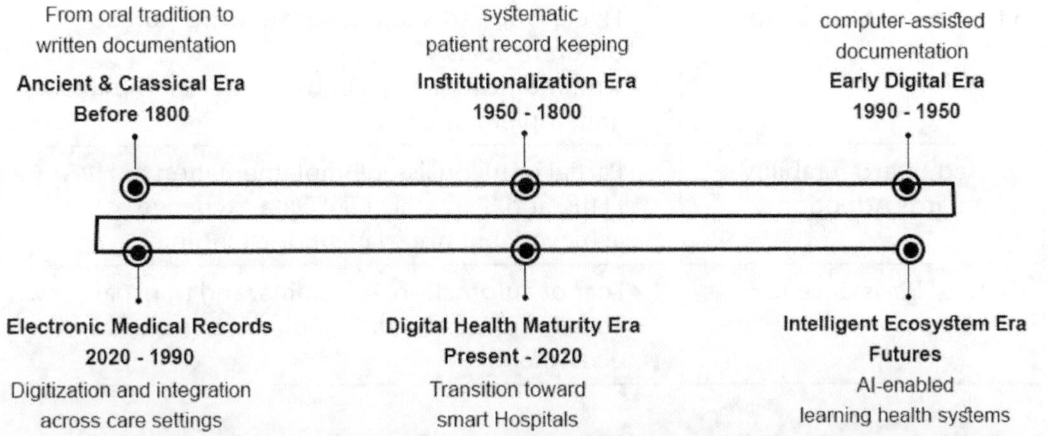

Figure 4.1 The shift in meaning

may exist, these systems often fail to communicate effectively with one another[6].

Furthermore, governance structures within hospitals are frequently either weak or reactive. This situation leads to ambiguity regarding data ownership and results in inconsistent decision-making processes. Even when technical systems are interconnected, the individuals responsible for managing and utilizing these systems, such as IT professionals, clinicians, and administrators, often pursue separate objectives rather than working toward shared goals.

Additional challenges include the incomplete adoption of interoperability standards and a prevailing cultural resistance to change. These factors collectively contribute to the ongoing difficulty in achieving genuine intelligence within health systems.

It is clear that technology alone is insufficient to create a truly intelligent ecosystem. Effective governance and organizational alignment are essential in transforming mere connectivity into meaningful cognition. Digital maturity and transformation frameworks emphasize leadership, governance, and culture as determinants of intelligent ecosystems[7](Table 4.1).

Table 4.1 Barriers in Creating an Intelligent Ecosystem

Fragmented Architecture	• Multiple systems, vendors, and databases without unified logic. Integration remains project-based, not principle-based.
Weak Governance Structures	• Lack of accountability, inconsistent data stewardship. • Policies exist on paper but not in daily operations.
Stakeholder Misalignment	• IT, clinical, and administrative teams pursue different goals. • Communication gaps between decision-makers and implementers.
Limited Interoperability Standards Adoption	• Partial or inconsistent implementation of HL7, FHIR, and SNOMED CT. "Data exchange" achieved, but not "data understanding".
Cultural Resistance to Change	• Fear of automation, role shifts, and transparency. • Technology is seen as a tool, not a shared ecosystem.

NOTE:

Technology can connect systems, but only governance and alignment can connect intelligence.

Artificial intelligence is significantly changing healthcare by improving the speed of diagnostics, advancing early disease detection, and supporting more accurate clinical decision-making[8]. AI tools, particularly those based on deep learning and natural language processing (NLP), are capable of analyzing medical images, electronic health record (EHR) data, and unstructured clinical notes[9]. These technologies help identify risks, suggest possible diagnoses, and extract information that may otherwise be overlooked due to time constraints. As a result, healthcare systems are moving from reactive approaches to more proactive and preventive care models[10]. NLP also streamlines documentation, reduces administrative workload, and uncovers valuable insights from free-text records. In addition, AI-driven decision support systems offer evidence-based recommendations, thereby enhancing patient safety and enabling more personalized care (Table 4.1).

AI is playing a central role in achieving semantic interoperability across healthcare organizations. By understanding clinical context, AI can map equivalent concepts between coding systems such as SNOMED CT, ICD-10, LOINC, and local terminologies. It can also convert unstructured notes into standardized data and identify inconsistencies during data exchange, ensuring that shared information maintains its intended meaning. When integrated with a Hospital Information System (HIS), chatbots extend the benefits of AI to patient engagement by providing triage support, personalized health guidance, administrative assistance, and post-discharge follow-up[11]. Collectively, these capabilities improve care quality, increase efficiency, reduce clinician workload, and foster more connected healthcare environments.

The integration of the Internet of Things (IoT) into HIS is transforming healthcare by delivering real-time data from wearable sensors, smart clinical equipment, real-time location systems (RTLS), home-based devices, and environmental monitors directly into the EHR. This creates a comprehensive and dynamic clinical picture[12]. IoT supports proactive care through remote monitoring of chronic diseases, automated adjustments in connected hospital devices, precise equipment tracking, and improved medication adherence. Operational efficiency is also enhanced by optimizing asset utilization, predicting equipment failures, and maintaining safe environmental conditions.

When combined with AI, IoT data becomes actionable intelligence, enabling early detection of patient deterioration, trend analysis, and personalized interventions. Future IoT ecosystems will depend on FHIR-based APIs, secure communication, and robust governance to ensure that device-generated data remains interoperable, private, and clinically relevant.

AI-powered smart surveillance, when integrated with health records, IoT sensors, and citywide digital infrastructure, has the potential to make public health systems more proactive and responsive[13]. Technologies such as thermal imaging, biometric sensors, and environmental data can help detect early signs of illness or distress in public spaces. With appropriate consent, AI can cross-reference these signals with individual health profiles and trigger personalized alerts or emergency responses. This system supports rapid interventions, from dispatching mobile medical units to guiding individuals toward safer behaviors, while also contributing anonymized data to national and global health platforms for outbreak detection and population health analytics. However, the use of such technologies requires strong ethical governance, privacy protections, transparent oversight, and public trust to ensure that health equity and personal dignity are maintained.

Predictive analytics is reshaping patient care and population health by leveraging historical, clinical, and real-time data to anticipate risks and guide proactive interventions. Machine learning models embedded in EHRs and HIS platforms can forecast complications, readmissions, or disease progression, enabling clinicians to adjust treatment plans and allocate resources efficiently. Risk stratification tools help identify individuals who require intensive monitoring or targeted support, particularly in chronic disease management. Integrated dashboards provide care teams with real-time views of patient cohorts and system-wide trends. This transition from reactive to anticipatory, data-driven decision-making leads to better outcomes, fewer avoidable hospitalizations, and supports value-based care.

Looking forward, predictive analytics will become even more effective when applied globally through unified health intelligence infrastructures. An international dashboard governed by the World Health Organization (WHO), built on FHIR interoperability, blockchain frameworks, and AI analytics, could aggregate anonymized data from hospitals, laboratories, mobile devices, and environmental sensors worldwide[14]. Such a system would serve as an early warning network for outbreaks, guide vaccine and resource deployment, inform public health policy, and support coordinated emergency responses. The inclusion of geospatial and environmental data would further enhance predictive models, while strict governance and privacy protections would ensure ethical use.

Blockchain technology provides a secure, decentralized, and tamper-resistant approach to managing health data by distributing records across multiple nodes rather than relying on a single server[15]. This structure makes unauthorized alterations nearly impossible and ensures data integrity and transparency. In healthcare, blockchain enables verifiable audit trails, tamper-evident validation of clinical documents, and fine-grained consent management through smart contracts that automatically enforce data-sharing rules. These features help build trust in multi-party environments, support compliance with regulations such as GDPR and HIPAA, and enhance patient control over health information. However, challenges remain, including scalability, integration with existing HIS/EHR systems, and regulatory uncertainties. Addressing these issues will require coordinated industry efforts, pilot projects, and the development of clear standards.

In future smart hospitals, cloud-native HIS platforms will replace traditional, hardware-dependent systems with agile, scalable architectures based on microservices, containerization, and cloud infrastructure. These platforms allow for continuous updates, high reliability, and on-demand resource scaling, reducing the burden of local IT maintenance. They also improve system resilience, support real-time data access, and integrate seamlessly with telehealth, remote monitoring, and wearable devices, making them well-suited for modern, distributed care models. Virtual care has expanded the role of HIS beyond hospital walls, enabling providers to conduct video visits, manage asynchronous consultations, incorporate home-generated health data, and coordinate care through patient portals and connected devices. Looking ahead, satellite technologies will further extend virtual care into remote and underserved regions by providing reliable connectivity, supporting IoT-enabled health monitoring, ensuring continuity during disasters, and enriching clinical decision-making with environmental and geospatial data.

Robots are expected to play a growing role in healthcare, functioning as intelligent extensions of HIS. These systems, which include delivery, disinfection, surgical, administrative, therapeutic, and home-assistance robots, will be able to read, update, and act on real-time clinical data. When integrated with HIS, robots can automate logistics, disinfect rooms, assist in surgery, prepare medications, support rehabilitation, conduct check-ins, monitor patient vitals, and enable virtual presence for clinicians or families. Humanoid and home-care robots will further enhance patient engagement, medication adherence, and remote monitoring, with behavioral and health data fed directly into the HIS for proactive care. Each robotic action will be logged and synchronized, improving safety, workflow efficiency, accuracy, and auditability. Ultimately, robots will become active participants in a continuous learning ecosystem, supporting clinicians, extending care beyond hospital walls, and generating high-quality data for analytics and decision-making.

The future of health insurance and claims management is moving toward fully digital, AI-driven, and personalized ecosystems. Real-time health data from wearables, HIS, and genomic profiles will inform individualized risk assessments, dynamic premiums, and proactive care recommendations. Blockchain-based smart contracts will automate claims by instantly validating services through FHIR-enabled HIS data, eliminating paperwork, delays, and fraud, while providing transparent audit trails and secure consent management. Insurers will shift from being reactive payers to preventive health partners, offering tailored interventions, intelligent prior authorizations, and incentives for healthy behaviors tracked through IoT devices. Global, portable insurance models will emerge through interoperable data standards and decentralized verification, supporting mobile populations and cross-border care. As claims automation becomes seamless, ethical safeguards, including protections against algorithmic bias, data misuse, and genetic discrimination, will be essential. Ultimately, insurance will serve not only as financial coverage but as an integrated, real-time enabler of long-term health, equity, and personalized well-being.

Enablers: Governance, Interoperability, and Stakeholder Alignment to Ensure Digital Transformation

To advance towards a more cognizant healthcare ecosystem, it is essential to focus on developing the appropriate enablers – those foundational elements that ensure sustainable intelligence within the sector.

- Governance Frameworks: Robust governance structures are necessary to define accountability and ensure that policies are closely aligned with desired outcomes.
- Interoperability: Systems should be designed with interoperability in mind from the outset, utilizing open standards and shared data languages to facilitate seamless integration.

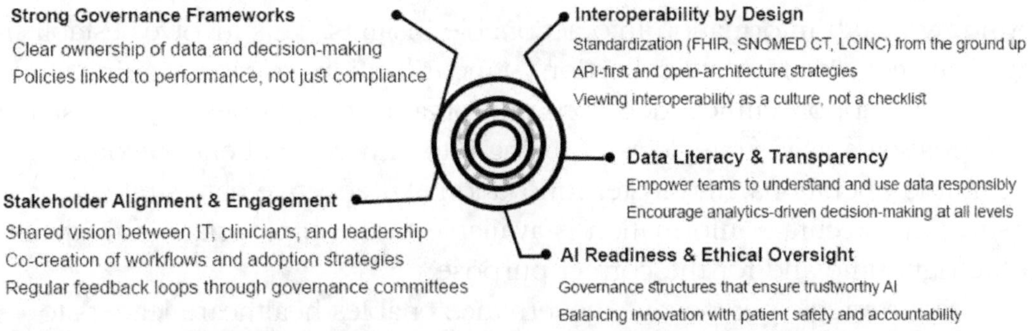

Figure 4.2 Building the foundation for a cognizant HIS ecosystem

- Stakeholder Alignment: It is important to bring together IT, clinical, and leadership teams under a unified vision for digital transformation.
- Data Literacy and Transparency: Empowering individuals with data literacy and providing transparent analytics helps to build trust across the organization.
- Ethical Oversight: Maintaining ethical oversight is critical to ensure that artificial intelligence is applied responsibly within healthcare settings.

By prioritizing these foundational elements, the healthcare sector can address existing barriers and move toward a more intelligent and sustainable future (Figure 4.2).

NOTE:

Governance aligns people. Interoperability aligns systems. Together, they make intelligence possible.

Health information governance and data strategy serve as essential links between the implementation of the Hospital Information System (HIS) and the realization of their long-term clinical, operational, and economic benefits[16]. Health information governance encompasses the policies, standards, roles, and processes that ensure health data remains available, accurate, secure, and appropriately used throughout its lifecycle. In HIS environments, governance must guarantee that data not only complies with regulatory and ethical standards but is also suitable for clinical use, accessible when required, and protected against misuse or breaches. Without such oversight, even advanced HIS solutions risk becoming fragmented, error-prone, or exposed to legal vulnerabilities.

Beyond governance, a comprehensive data strategy is necessary to transform raw health information into actionable insights. This involves establishing clear methods for data collection, standardization, storage, sharing, and analysis to support clinical decisions and organizational objectives. Hospitals must treat data as a strategic asset, using it to enhance patient outcomes, streamline operations, and foster innovation. An effective data strategy ensures that accurate information is available to the appropriate individuals at the right time and for the correct purpose.

From a strategic perspective, governance enables healthcare leaders to depend on HIS data for evidence-based planning, resource allocation, and performance monitoring. By upholding data quality and consistency, governance ensures that dashboards, reports, and analytics accurately reflect operational and clinical realities[17]. This reliability allows hospital executives and policymakers to make informed decisions regarding staffing, budgeting, service expansion, population health, and compliance, thereby positioning HIS data as a valuable asset for organizational development and quality improvement.

Interoperability and consistency across systems and facilities are equally important. HIS environments frequently interact with laboratories, pharmacies, government databases, research systems, and patient portals. Inconsistent data definitions and formats can lead to miscommunication and errors. Therefore, governance and strategy should incorporate interoperability frameworks, semantic alignment, and master data management to ensure that patient data remains usable and meaningful at every point of care.

A digital governance committee forms a fundamental component of an effective governance structure. This committee provides oversight, direction, and accountability, establishing overarching policies, standards, and strategic direction within the healthcare organization. It creates a transparent decision-making framework that integrates diverse stakeholder perspectives and offers mechanisms for resolving complex data challenges. Through its oversight, governance committees help align HIS capabilities with operational and clinical needs, mitigate risks, improve data quality, and reinforce accountability across departments. As such, these committees are critical to developing a mature and sustainable governance environment[18].

A robust governance structure depends on clearly defined roles and responsibilities to ensure that policies are consistently applied throughout the organization. Key roles include:

- Chief Data Officer (CDO): Provides strategic leadership and ensures data governance aligns with institutional priorities.
- Data Stewards: Maintain data quality and act as the operational link between data users and policymakers.
- Privacy Officers: Protect patient information by monitoring compliance with privacy regulations such as HIPAA or GDPR.

By explicitly assigning these roles, organizations ensure that HIS governance is actively managed, monitored, and continuously improved.

Effective data and digital governance are fundamental to achieving compliance. Compliance ensures that HIS operations are legally sound, ethically responsible, and aligned with industry best practices[19]. This reduces risk, builds trust, and supports the safe and effective delivery of healthcare. Compliance is not solely about avoiding penalties; it also involves safeguarding patient rights, promoting data transparency, and maintaining organizational accountability in a digital health environment.

Operationally, failure to comply can result in data breaches and the unauthorized release of sensitive patient information. Such incidents compromise patient privacy and trust, and may lead to harm, including misdiagnosis, identity theft, or social stigma. Furthermore, publicized compliance failures can damage an institution's reputation, affect partnerships, and reduce patient engagement with digital health services. Ultimately, non-compliance undermines the integrity and safety of healthcare delivery.

In future healthcare environments, interoperability extends beyond the technical exchange of data[20]. It encompasses the ability of diverse applications, devices, platforms, and institutions to communicate, interpret, and act on shared information securely and meaningfully. Modern hospitals depend on a range of digital tools, including electronic health records (EHRs), laboratory systems, imaging platforms, decision-support engines, cloud services, and wearable devices. Interoperability ensures these systems function cohesively. It also enables secure, real-time communication with public health agencies, pharmacies, insurers, community care providers, and other hospitals. This seamless connectivity supports a continuously learning health ecosystem, allowing information to follow the patient and facilitating timely, coordinated, and effective care.

Semantic interoperability ensures that the meaning of exchanged data remains consistent across different contexts, systems, and decision-making environments. This capability transforms raw data into trusted clinical intelligence, supporting reliable automated reasoning, predictive modeling, and evidence-based care. It enables healthcare providers to access a complete, accurate, and contextualized patient record across all care settings, from emergency departments to inpatient services, outpatient clinics, rehabilitation, and home monitoring.

Types of Interoperability in Smart Healthcare

1. Foundational Interoperability

   It enables basic data exchange between systems; one can send information, and another can receive it, but it does not guarantee interpretation. This level provides minimal connectivity but requires human intervention to interpret meaning. It is a necessary starting point but insufficient for automation, decision support, or AI-driven workflows.
2. Structural Interoperability

   Structural interoperability applies standardized data formats, message structures, and field organization (such as HL7 v2, CDA, or XML schemas). It ensures that receiving systems can parse data correctly, placing values in the correct fields and storing them appropriately. This level enables automated processing and consistent display of data across interfaces.
3. Semantic Interoperability

   Semantic interoperability ensures that the meaning of clinical data remains intact across all systems. It uses standardized terminologies (SNOMED CT, ICD-11, LOINC, and RxNorm) so that diagnoses, observations, and treatments carry the same interpretation everywhere. This is essential for decision support, analytics, and accurate, coordinated patient care.
4. Organizational Interoperability

   Organizational interoperability aligns the policies, legal agreements, processes, and governance across institutions. Even when technologies connect successfully, interoperability can still fail if organizations have conflicting workflows, unclear responsibilities, or restrictive data-sharing rules. This level ensures collaboration is technically feasible, operationally aligned, and legally compliant.

Interoperability and semantic alignment are not optional; they are core enablers of a modern, intelligent Hospital Information System (HIS). They create the infrastructure necessary for real-time analytics, AI-driven support, cross-institution collaboration, and long-term system-wide improvement. When implemented effectively, they transform health information from isolated data points into shared clinical intelligence, driving safer, faster, and smarter decision-making across the entire healthcare ecosystem.

Stakeholder management in future smart hospitals requires a shift from traditional, linear engagement practices toward dynamic, continuous, and intelligence-driven collaboration. Stakeholder engagement is "simple in concept but difficult in practice", largely because hospitals are complex socio-technical environments where expectations, workflows, and pressures constantly evolve. In smart hospitals, where AI, automation, interoperability, and real-time data streams shape daily operations, the stakes of engagement become even higher. Stakeholders are no longer just system users; they are co-creators of a learning, adaptive ecosystem where their feedback and interactions directly influence system intelligence and performance.

From Tools to Ecosystem – Enhancing Cognitive Capacity

Integration has marked a significant milestone in hospital operations; however, it represents only an initial step in a broader transformation. For many years, electronic medical records (EMRs) have functioned primarily as reactive systems. These platforms collect and store data, issuing alerts only after clinical events have occurred. As a result, healthcare organizations have accumulated substantial amounts of data, yet meaningful insights have often remained limited[21].

The current landscape is shifting toward intelligent decision support. Integrated data systems now facilitate more advanced capabilities, including predictive analytics, workflow optimization, and real-time clinical alerts. This transition moves the focus from simply reacting to clinical events to anticipating them. Importantly, these advancements are designed to augment, not replace, the expertise of clinicians. Artificial intelligence assists in identifying patterns that may not be immediately apparent, supporting timely, evidence-based, and contextually relevant decisions. The true transformation lies in progressing from systems that merely record information to those that can interpret and understand it.

Table 4.2 Reactive Systems vs Proactive and Cognizant Systems

Reactive Systems	Proactive and Cognizant Systems
Yesterday's EMR: Data-Rich, Insight-Poor * Data captured but rarely analyzed in real time. * Systems respond *after* an event (alerts after errors, reports after discharge). * Clinicians spend time searching for information instead of interpreting it.	Tomorrow's HIS: Cognizant and Predictive * Integrated data across departments and devices. * Predictive analytics detect risk *before* it happens. * Clinical decision support provides real-time guidance. * AI enhances – not replaces – clinical reasoning.

Presently, most EMR environments continue to operate as reactive systems. While they are capable of collecting large volumes of data, they seldom convert this information into actionable, real-time insights. Typically, analysis occurs only after clinical events, resulting in delayed alerts, retrospective reporting, and clinicians dedicating significant time to data retrieval rather than interpretation for decision-making.

In contrast, the next generation of hospital information systems (HIS) aims to establish proactive and perceptive environments. These systems integrate data seamlessly across departments and devices, providing a unified and continuous view of each patient's journey. Predictive analytics are employed to identify potential risks before they arise, while clinical decision support tools offer real-time guidance at the point of care. Artificial intelligence serves to enhance clinical reasoning, equipping healthcare professionals with timely insights that contribute to improved safety, efficiency, and patient outcomes (Table 4.2).

NOTE:

Intelligence in healthcare is not automation. It's an amplification of human judgment.

The integration of artificial intelligence and decision support tools within health systems requires a steadfast commitment to ethical standards. It is essential that advancements in intelligence do not compromise ethical considerations.

Transparency is fundamental; it enables both clinicians and patients to understand the reasoning behind decisions, rather than merely observing

Figure 4.3 From tools to ecosystem

the outcomes. Accountability is equally important, as it guarantees ongoing human oversight and clearly defines responsibility for the design and application of these systems. Addressing bias is also critical, since data often reflect human behaviors that may perpetuate inequality unless deliberate corrective measures are taken.

The principles of transparency, accountability, and fairness are central to building trust in technology. In healthcare, intelligence that is not guided by ethics does not represent progress; rather, it introduces significant risk (Figure 4.3).

Here are key elements in compliance in future smart hospitals:

1. Digital Patient Rights and Autonomous Data Privacy

   In the evolving landscape of smart hospitals, patient privacy is shifting from traditional protection of personal health information to a broader framework of digital patient rights. This approach emphasizes individual control over how personal data is managed and shared across artificial intelligence systems, interconnected devices, and external healthcare networks.

   Smart hospitals are required to protect patient identities and sensitive information throughout various digital environments, including cloud platforms, Internet of Things (IoT) medical devices, remote monitoring solutions, and AI-driven analytics. Ensuring compliance involves implementing real-time consent management, providing clear explanations of data usage, and adhering to international standards such as the General Data Protection Regulation (GDPR), the Health Insurance Portability and Accountability Act (HIPAA), and new national regulations related to artificial intelligence.

Automated systems must be in place to enable patients to access, update, restrict, or withdraw their data-sharing preferences at any time through secure, intelligent portals. This comprehensive privacy model is designed to uphold patient autonomy, minimize risks associated with algorithmic decision-making, and maintain trust in an environment where care is increasingly personalized and data-driven.

2. Intelligent Security and Zero-Trust Access Control

   As smart hospitals evolve into highly interconnected environments, traditional role-based access control methods are no longer adequate. The future of compliance in these settings depends on adopting zero-trust security principles, which require that every access request is continuously verified. This verification is based on several factors, including user identity, contextual information, device integrity, and behavioral patterns.

   Key components of effective access governance include multifactor authentication, biometric validation, encrypted data transmission, and ongoing monitoring. These elements collectively form a robust foundation for managing access intelligently within the hospital ecosystem.

   Automated anomaly detection systems play a critical role by identifying suspicious activities, such as insider threats, and enabling immediate containment measures. It is essential that security protocols extend beyond central systems to encompass edge devices, robotic platforms, diagnostic equipment, and cloud-based clinical solutions.

   By integrating adaptive, AI-driven security measures into every workflow, smart hospitals are able to safeguard patient data, maintain operational resilience, and uphold compliance across increasingly complex digital environments.

3. Standardized Clinical Language and Semantic Interoperability

   Modern smart hospitals increasingly depend on semantic interoperability. This approach ensures that clinical data is not only standardized, but also machine-readable, context-aware, and suitable for use in advanced analytics and decision-support systems.

   To achieve compliance, hospitals must consistently implement global standards such as ICD-11, SNOMED CT, LOINC, and HL7 FHIR. In addition, automated validation tools are essential for maintaining documentation accuracy across both human-entered and device-generated data streams.

Intelligent coding assistants and real-time validation algorithms support clinicians in documenting information efficiently, while maintaining high data quality. Through such standardization, artificial intelligence models receive dependable inputs, and hospitals are able to exchange data seamlessly across regional health networks.

As a result, clinical, operational, and financial decisions are based on information that is both trusted and comparable. In environments where automation and intelligence rely on clean, structured data, semantic quality becomes a fundamental compliance requirement.

4. Lifecycle Data Stewardship, Retention, and Intelligent Legal Hold

   In modern smart hospital environments, data retention has evolved into comprehensive lifecycle stewardship. Organizations are now responsible for managing clinical, operational, and sensor-generated data from the point of creation through to final disposal.

   To maintain compliance, it is essential to establish clear guidelines regarding the retention periods for digital records, imaging archives, IoT telemetry, and AI training datasets. These guidelines must also address secure archiving methods and specify the appropriate timing for data destruction.

   Intelligent legal hold systems play a critical role by automatically identifying legal or regulatory events. When such events occur, these systems immediately halt any data deletion processes, ensuring that all relevant information, including logs, device outputs, and records of algorithmic decisions, is preserved.

   As the volume of data continues to increase within smart hospitals, automated governance tools are necessary to uphold legal, ethical, and operational standards. These tools also help optimize storage resources and minimize institutional risk.

5. Continuous Auditability, Traceability, and Algorithmic Accountability

   In the evolving landscape of smart hospitals, compliance requires comprehensive visibility into both human actions and machine-generated decisions. It is essential to maintain continuous audit trails that record every access, modification, clinical order, device action, and algorithmic recommendation in real time. These records are critical for supporting regulatory reviews, identifying anomalies, and maintaining trust in clinical environments where artificial intelligence is integrated into workflows.

Advanced monitoring tools play a vital role by tracking user behavior, automatically detecting policy violations, and providing compliance officers with clear dashboards. Equally significant is the need for algorithmic traceability. This involves demonstrating how an AI system arrived at a particular conclusion, identifying the data it utilized, and assessing whether bias or drift influenced its output. Such transparency is fundamental for ensuring accountability, supporting ethical AI deployment, and aligning smart hospitals with emerging global regulations for safe and responsible digital healthcare.

Ethical considerations in digital health extend well beyond traditional data protection. They require a principled approach to the use, sharing, and interpretation of patient information within increasingly intelligent systems. At the core of this approach is the ethical mandate to use health data fairly and justly, ensuring that information is processed solely for legitimate purposes that support patient care, safety, and equitable service delivery.

As smart hospitals increasingly depend on automation and predictive analytics, it is crucial to design systems that prevent discrimination, stigmatization, or unequal treatment resulting from biased datasets or algorithmic behavior. Upholding dignity, fairness, and inclusivity must be a foundational requirement in every digital interaction.

Secondary uses of health data, such as research, population health analytics, and training AI models, provide significant value but also introduce new ethical challenges. Even when data is de-identified, repurposing it beyond its original context may conflict with patient expectations and autonomy. Many patients remain unaware that their clinical data may be used to develop commercial algorithms, train machine learning tools, or support initiatives they have not explicitly approved.

In future digital ecosystems, ethical governance must balance innovation with responsibility. This involves enforcing transparency, establishing effective oversight mechanisms, and, when necessary, obtaining renewed or dynamic consent for secondary uses of data.

Transparency and accountability are essential pillars of ethical digital health. Smart hospitals must implement consent processes that are clear, accessible, and meaningful, rather than obscured by legal complexity or presented as unchangeable defaults. Digital systems should incorporate tools that document consent, track data usage across applications and algorithms, and enable patients to review, modify, or revoke permissions.

Beyond legal compliance, ethical digital health environments foster trust by treating patients as informed partners in the data lifecycle. This culture of openness and respect enhances the credibility of digital innovation and ensures that the future of healthcare remains responsible, human-centered, and aligned with societal values.

Future of HIS as a Learning Health Ecosystem – AI-Enabled Smart and Responsive EMR/HIS

Clinicians, patients, administrators, and IT teams collectively form the core of a learning health ecosystem. Their experiences, feedback, and collaboration are essential for driving meaningful transformation within healthcare organizations. By sharing real-world challenges and successes, each group contributes to a continuous learning cycle. These interactions generate practical knowledge, shaping the evolution of systems and the delivery of care. While technology serves as an important enabler, it is ultimately human insight, creativity, and judgment that drive ongoing improvement.

Processes provide the necessary structure to transform daily activities into repeatable and scalable learning cycles. Standardized workflows ensure consistent data capture, reliable measurement of outcomes, and reinforcement of best practices throughout the organization[22]. By integrating learning into routine operations, health systems can systematically gather evidence, test new approaches, and implement changes efficiently. These processes establish a predictable rhythm that supports continuous learning.

High-quality, interoperable data is fundamental to the learning ecosystem. When data moves accurately and seamlessly across departments, devices, and care settings, it creates a unified perspective on patient care and system performance. Reliable data not only supports clinical decision-making but also ensures that insights derived from analytics are both trustworthy and actionable. In a learning health system, data is regarded as a strategic asset that drives ongoing improvement, rather than merely a byproduct of care.

Insights are produced when analytics convert raw data into actionable intelligence in real time. This process involves identifying patterns, predicting risks, and highlighting opportunities to enhance patient outcomes or operational efficiency. Advanced analytics and artificial intelligence are critical in processing large volumes of information that are beyond human capacity to interpret alone[23]. These insights enable clinicians and leaders to make informed decisions and respond proactively.

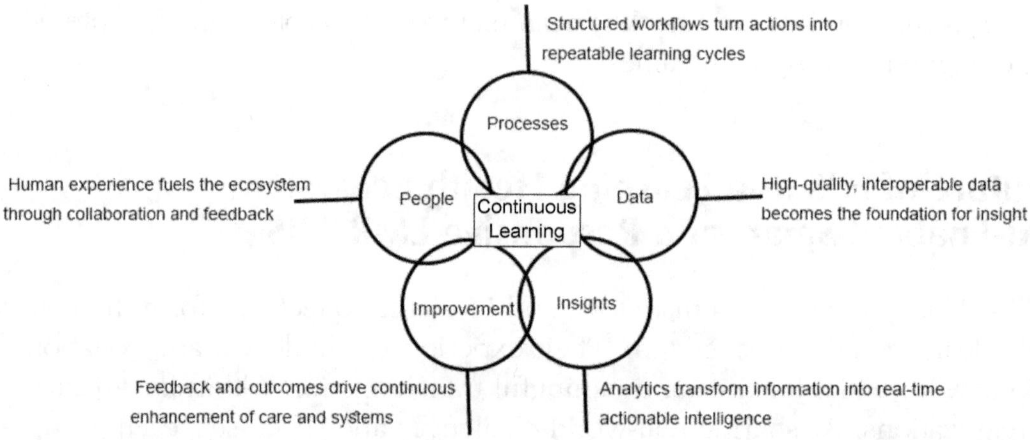

Figure 4.4 Future of HIS as a learning health ecosystem

Improvement serves as both the outcome and the ongoing driver of the learning ecosystem. Feedback loops, supported by data, insights, and human experience, facilitate the continuous enhancement of care delivery, workflows, and systems. As improvements are implemented, they generate new data and experiences, which are then reintegrated into the learning cycle. This self-reinforcing process ensures that the organization becomes progressively more effective, safe, and knowledgeable over time (Figure 4.4).

NOTE:

The ecosystem evolves with every interaction, learning, adapting, and growing smarter over time.

To achieve accurate, comprehensive, and interconnected data across all points of care, it is essential to establish a solid data foundation. Integrating disparate systems and standardizing data enables the creation of a digital infrastructure where information can move intelligently and securely. This approach lays the groundwork for leveraging artificial intelligence, machine learning, and analytics to transform data into actionable insights. The ultimate goal is to develop a system capable of recognizing patterns, predicting risks, and supporting clinical reasoning, while also providing a responsive and adaptive user interface.

A Layered Model for Building an Intelligent Hospital Information System (HIS) The following layered model outlines the structured progression necessary to develop an intelligent and responsive Hospital Information System (HIS). Each layer builds upon the previous one, illustrating that advanced digital capabilities depend on strong foundational elements. Collectively, these layers guide the transformation from basic data capture to a fully adaptive and user-centered health ecosystem.

1. Data and Foundation Layer
   This foundational layer encompasses all core clinical and operational data, as well as the technical infrastructure required to store and manage it. High-quality, reliable, and well-structured data is indispensable. Without this solid base, advanced functions such as analytics and automation cannot operate safely or effectively.
2. Integration and Interoperability
   The next layer focuses on ensuring seamless data flow across systems, departments, and devices. Effective integration and interoperability enable the creation of unified patient records and eliminate information silos. This capability allows the HIS to function as a cohesive environment, rather than a collection of isolated tools. It also reduces errors, supports continuity of care, and underpins coordinated clinical workflows.
3. Intelligence and Analytics
   Building upon the previous layers, this stage involves transforming raw data into meaningful insights. Through reporting, dashboards, decision-support tools, and advanced analytics such as machine learning, the HIS evolves from a passive repository of information to an active generator of clinical and operational intelligence. This advancement facilitates earlier risk detection, improved planning, and more informed decision-making.
4. Experience and Response
   The top layer represents the user-facing aspect of the system. It includes the interfaces used by clinicians, the alerts and recommendations provided, and the system's ability to adapt to various contexts and needs. A well-designed experience layer enhances clinical reasoning, improves usability, and ensures timely, relevant responses for both clinicians and patients.

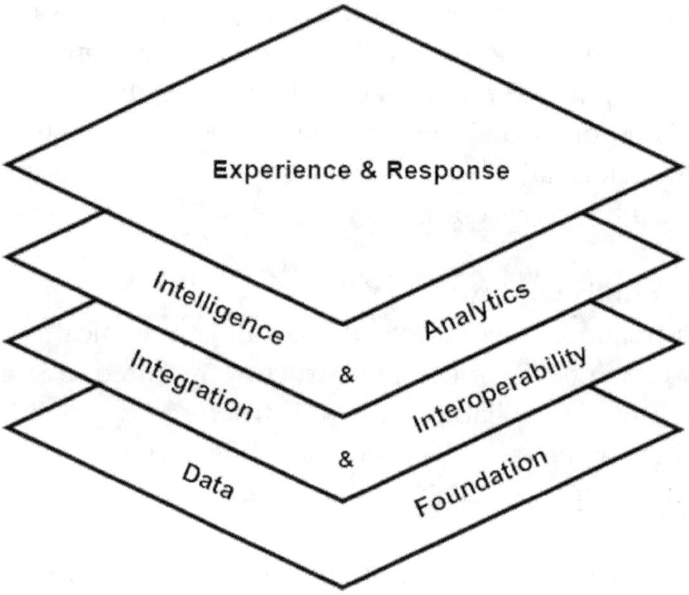

Figure 4.5 Future of HIS as a learning health ecosystem

Conclusion

This model underscores a fundamental principle: Advanced HIS capabilities are only possible with strong foundational layers. Successful digital transformation requires investment in clean data, robust integration, and meaningful analytics before pursuing intelligent and adaptive user experiences. Adhering to this structured approach ensures that the Hospital Information System (HIS) develops into a truly responsive and learning health ecosystem (Figure 4.5).

NOTE:

A Smart and Responsive EMR is not one system. It's an ecosystem of layers that sense, think, and act together.

Hospital Information systems (HIS's) are expected to depend more extensively on digital technologies to provide care in the future. As a result, the volume, complexity, and sensitivity of health data will increase significantly.

Expanding Uses of Patient Data
Patient data will no longer serve solely as a resource for individual treatment. It will become fundamental to a range of functions, including:

- Population health management
- Financial reporting
- Quality improvement initiatives
- Medical research
- Public health surveillance

Given this heightened reliance on data, it is essential to adopt a structured approach to the governance, protection, and strategic use of health information. Health information governance will therefore play a critical role in ensuring that data is managed effectively and responsibly across all areas of healthcare.

HIS Project Success in Smart Future Healthcare Ecosystem

The Strategic Role of Governance in HIS Projects

Implementing a Health Information System (HIS) Project Governance Framework in a future smart hospital requires recognizing governance as a strategic foundation, not merely an administrative function[24]. As hospitals transition into highly connected, AI-enabled environments, the quality and integrity of governance will have a direct impact on the performance of HIS projects. Establishing a governance program demands early executive sponsorship, a defined strategic purpose, and a governance structure that supports continuous learning and digital transformation. Leadership commitment is essential to provide authority, allocate resources, and ensure visibility, making governance a hospital-wide priority from the outset of HIS implementation.

Aligning Governance with Digital Maturity

A robust HIS Project Governance Framework must be purposefully aligned with the hospital's vision for digital maturity and the broader requirements of the digital healthcare ecosystem, rather than focusing solely on smart hospital capabilities. This alignment involves defining a governance purpose that addresses clinical safety, operational efficiency, regulatory compliance, and readiness for AI integration. Establishing the governance structure typically includes forming dedicated bodies such as a Data Governance Board and a Healthcare Ecosystem Oversight Committee.

Integration of Governance into HIS Implementation

For an HIS Project Governance Program to support the success of future smart hospitals, it must be fully integrated into all HIS implementation activities. Data governance should play an active role in guiding system configuration, interface design, workflow mapping, testing, and training[25]. Clearly defined roles and responsibilities form the operational backbone that translates governance policies into consistent practice. This includes developing formal role descriptions, assigning stewardship duties, and establishing escalation and decision-making pathways to ensure accountability and minimize ambiguity. These structures also prepare the hospital for advanced capabilities such as real-time monitoring, AI-driven recommendations, predictive analytics, and automated safety checks, all of which depend on reliable, well-governed data.

In smart hospitals, where automation, interoperability, and AI applications depend on consistent data standards, core policies regarding data access, data quality, classification, retention, privacy, and security become increasingly vital.

Sustaining Leadership Support and Demonstrating Value

Ongoing leadership support is necessary throughout the governance journey, particularly as smart hospitals increasingly rely on advanced digital capabilities. Demonstrating governance as a strategic enabler, through clear business cases, early achievements, and regular communication, helps leadership understand how governance reduces risk, improves care quality, and strengthens organizational intelligence. Integrating governance into existing committees and oversight structures normalizes the practice, while executive dashboards and progress reports keep leadership engaged in monitoring governance performance.

Building a Foundation for Advanced Capabilities

The success of HIS projects in future smart hospitals will depend on more than technology alone. A mature governance framework provides the structure, clarity, and accountability necessary to ensure data integrity, safe workflows, and the effective deployment of advanced capabilities such as AI, predictive modeling, and automation. By embedding governance into the foundation of HIS implementation, hospitals position themselves to evolve into intelligent, learning ecosystems that support continuous improvement and deliver high-quality patient care.

Stakeholder Management and the Core Interaction Model (CIM)

Stakeholder management is an area where the Core Interaction Model (CIM) offers distinct advantages. Unlike traditional implementation models, CIM treats HIS projects as ongoing cycles of observation, implementation, and qualification, making stakeholder input essential at every stage. Failures in HIS projects are often attributed to non-technical factors such as resistance to change, insufficient engagement, and poor communication[26]. CIM addresses these challenges by embedding stakeholder collaboration into its core processes. As smart hospitals increasingly depend on automation, proactive decision support, and AI-driven workflows, CIM ensures that human expertise, professional judgment, and frontline insights remain central to system development.

In smart hospitals, stakeholder roles are more dynamic and interconnected. Physicians serve as validators of clinical algorithms, administrators act as data quality stewards, and nurses contribute real-time process intelligence through continuous feedback systems. In this environment, identifying stakeholders, understanding their expectations, and maintaining structured communication channels are essential. CIM enhances this by transforming engagement from a discrete project phase into an ongoing ecosystem function. It enables hospital leaders to treat stakeholder interactions as operational data, signals that inform system refinement, model recalibration, workflow redesign, and governance decisions.

CIM aligns with the digital maturity trajectory of smart hospitals. As these environments become more predictive, autonomous, and interconnected, the consequences of neglecting stakeholder concerns increase significantly. Resistance to change or unclear communication can erode trust, hinder adoption, or disrupt AI-driven processes. The cyclical nature of CIM ensures continuous alignment among people, processes, data, and technology. It transforms traditional feedback mechanisms, such as surveys and user groups, into real-time, intelligence-supported processes that enable rapid correction, responsive design, and shared ownership.

The future of stakeholder management in smart hospitals is closely linked to the principles of the Core Interaction Model. CIM provides the structure and clarity required to navigate complex digital transformations while keeping human experience central. It establishes engagement as a strategic asset that supports continuous learning, builds trust, accelerates adoption, and ensures that smart hospitals remain aligned with the needs and values of their stakeholders.

Project Management in Smart Hospitals:

Project management in future smart hospitals will develop into a systems-driven, AI-supported discipline, reflecting the broader shift in project management from process-heavy approaches to principle-based, outcome-oriented value delivery. According to PMBOK, project management is moving toward a systems perspective, where projects are part of a larger value network that advances organizational strategy and long-term capability building. In smart hospitals, where IoT infrastructures, AI-driven diagnostics, robotic systems, and autonomous workflows interact continuously, project managers must coordinate interdependent components rather than simply oversee tasks. HIS projects in these settings become complex socio-technical transformations, requiring project managers to anticipate system interactions, emerging risks, and the need for ongoing adaptation.

AI-enabled project intelligence will redefine planning, monitoring, and decision-making. Modern project environments require adaptability, rapid decision cycles, and continuous learning. In future smart hospitals, AI will support these needs by providing predictive risk modeling, automated scheduling, real-time resource forecasting, and sentiment analysis of stakeholder communications[27]. Rather than manually compiling reports, project managers will utilize AI dashboards that synthesize project data, user feedback, workflow bottlenecks, and readiness indicators, enabling early issue detection and faster alignment with project objectives. AI will also facilitate the simulation of configuration changes, workflow redesigns, or system upgrades before their implementation in live hospital operations.

HIS projects in digital hospitals must coordinate the efforts of clinicians, data scientists, biomedical engineers, cybersecurity teams, patients, and regulatory bodies, many of whom interact with intelligent systems daily. AI-assisted engagement tools will monitor user sentiment, track behavioral adoption, and identify shifts in stakeholder influence or resistance. This approach aligns with CIM's focus on continuously monitoring changes in stakeholder attitudes and engagement effectiveness throughout the project lifecycle. Project managers will be able to make data-informed engagement decisions in real time, reducing friction and improving adoption.

By leveraging machine learning, Project Management Offices (PMOs) will identify patterns across multiple HIS implementations, predict potential failure points, optimize training plans, and recommend governance adjustments. This evolution will shift project delivery from reactive problem-solving to a learning ecosystem.

The Core Interaction Model (CIM) is well-suited to this future vision of project management. Its cyclical structure of observation, implementation, and qualification is critical. In smart hospitals, where systems are designed to learn and evolve, CIM serves as the operational backbone that keeps HIS projects aligned with real-time clinical needs. As PMBOK emphasizes the role of projects as agents of change that must integrate stakeholder needs throughout the value chain, CIM operationalizes this by embedding continuous feedback loops, cross-functional collaboration, and iterative refinement, turning stakeholder insights and system intelligence into actionable improvements. CIM transforms HIS implementation from a finite project into continuous value delivery, consistent with the modern project ecosystem.

References

1. Rajaei O, Lashkari B, Kazemi A, Memari M. Smart hospital: A systematic review of academic and industrial perspectives. *Int J Med Inform.* 2024;184:105386.
2. Levina A, Shklyar A, Martynov K, et al. Towards smart hospital: Integrating smart infrastructure solutions. *Digit Health.* 2024;12:1–11.
3. AHIMA. *Health Information Management: Concepts, Principles, and Practice.* 5th ed. American Health Information Management Association; 2012.
4. Health Level Seven International. *HL7 Version 2 Product Suite.* HL7; 2012.
5. Cresswell KM, Sheikh A. Organizational issues in the implementation and adoption of health information technology innovations: An interpretative review. *Int J Med Inform.* 2013;82(5):e73–e86. doi:10.1016/j.ijmedinf.2012.10.007.

6. Adler-Milstein J, Pfeifer E. Information blocking: Is it occurring and what policy strategies can address it? *Milbank Q.* 2017;95(1):117–135. doi:10.1111/1468-0009.12247.
7. Westerman G , Bonnet D, McAfee A. *Leading Digital: Turning Technology into Business Transformation.* Harvard Business Review Press; 2014.
8. Topol EJ. High-performance medicine: The convergence of human and artificial intelligence. *Nat Med.* 2019;25(1):44–56. doi:10.1038/s41591-018-0300-7
9. Wang Y , Wang L, Rastegar-Mojarad M, et al. Clinical information extraction applications: A literature review. *J Biomed Inform.* 2018;77:34–49. doi:10.1016/j.jbi.2017.11.011.
10. Obermeyer Z, Emanuel EJ. Predicting the future - big data, machine learning, and clinical medicine. *N Engl J Med.* 2016;375(13):1216–1219. doi:10.1056/NEJMp1606181
11. Laranjo L, Dunn AG, Tong HL, et al. Conversational agents in healthcare: A systematic review. *J Am Med Inform Assoc.* 2018;25(9):1248–1258. doi:10.1093/jamia/ocy072
12. Kelly JT, Campbell KL, Gong E, Scuffham P. The internet of things: impact and implications for healthcare delivery. *J Med Internet Res.* 2020 Nov 10;22(11):E20135. doi:10.2196/20135
13. Salathé M, Bengtsson L, Bodnar TJ, et al. Digital epidemiology. *PLoS Comput Biol.* 2012;8(7):E1002616. doi:10.1371/journal.pcbi.1002616
14. World Health Organization. *Ethics and Governance of Artificial Intelligence for Health.* WHO; 2021.
15. Agbo CC, Mahmoud QH, Eklund JM. Blockchain technology in healthcare: A systematic review. *Healthcare (Basel).* 2019 Apr 4;7(2):56. doi:10.3390/healthcare7020056
16. Smallwood RF. *Information Governance: Concepts, Strategies, and Best Practices.* 2nd ed. Wiley; 2019.
17. Batini C, Scannapieco M. *Data Quality: Concepts, Methodologies and Techniques.* Springer; 2006.
18. Kane GC, Palmer D, Phillips AN, Kiron D, Buckley N. *Strategy, Not Technology, Drives Digital Transformation.* MIT Sloan Management Review and Deloitte Insights; 2015.
19. Rumbold JM, Pierscionek B. The effect of the general data protection regulation on medical research. *J Med Internet Res.* 2017 Feb 24;19(2):E47. doi:10.2196/jmir.7108
20. HIMSS. *Interoperability in Healthcare: Definition and Policy Overview.* HIMSS; 2020.
21. Raghupathi W, Raghupathi V. Big data analytics in healthcare: Promise and potential. *Health Inf Sci Syst.* 2014 Feb 7;2:3. doi:10.1186/2047-2501-2-3
22. Obermeyer Z, Powers B, Vogeli C, Mullainathan S. Dissecting racial bias in an algorithm used to manage the health of populations. *Science.* 2019;366(6464):447–453. doi:10.1126/science.aax2342
23. Kaye J, Whitley EA, Lund D, et al. Dynamic consent: A patient interface for twenty-first century research. *Eur J Hum Genet.* 2015;23(2):141–146.

24. Weill P, Ross JW. *IT Governance: How Top Performers Manage IT Decision Rights for Superior Results.* Harvard Business School Press; 2004.
25. Greenhalgh T, Wherton J, Papoutsi C, et al. Beyond adoption: A new framework for theorizing and evaluating nonadoption, abandonment, and challenges to the scale-up, spread, and sustainability of health and care technologies. *J Med Internet Res.* 2017 Nov 1;19(11):E367. doi:10.2196/jmir.8775
26. Heeks R. Health information systems: Failure, success and improvisation. *Int J Med Inform.* 2006;75(2):125–137.
27. Serrador P, Pinto JK. Does agile work? A quantitative analysis of agile project success. *Int J Proj Manag.* 2015;33(5):1040–1051.

Glossary

A

Access Control: Mechanisms that restrict user access to data based on roles or permissions (example RBAC) to protect patient privacy and maintain compliance.

Accountability: Ensuring individuals and teams are responsible for actions related to HIS operations, data handling, and clinical documentation.

Accuracy (Data Accuracy): The degree to which data correctly describes the real-world event or patient condition.

Adaptive Delivery: An iterative approach allowing HIS project teams to adjust scope and execution as new information emerges.

Adaptive Ecosystem: A digitally enabled healthcare environment capable of learning, evolving, and adjusting workflows, intelligence, and operations in response to real-time clinical, operational, and environmental signals.

Agile: A flexible, iterative project framework emphasizing collaboration, rapid delivery, and ongoing adaptation.

Asset (Health Information as an Asset): The concept that data has measurable operational, clinical, and strategic value.

Autonomous Workflows: AI-driven, self-managing processes that adjust operational steps without human intervention (example automated triage, robotic tasks).

B–C

Change Management: Structured methods to help individuals and teams transition through HIS-related changes.

CIM - Core Interaction Model: A continuous cycle integrating observation, implementation, and qualification to guide HIS project success.

Clinical Decision Support (CDS): Tools providing evidence-based recommendations to improve clinical quality and safety.

Clinical Documentation: The structured recording of patient information, essential for care, billing, analytics, and compliance.

Cloud Computing: Using remote servers for data storage, analytics, and HIS hosting.

Coding: Transforming diagnoses, procedures, and clinical findings into standardized codes (example ICD-10, SNOMED CT).

Cognizant Healthcare Ecosystem: A learning, sensing, and adaptive hospital environment where systems, people, and processes collaboratively interpret and act on data.

Compliance (Legal & Regulatory): Adherence to laws such as GDPR, HIPAA, data retention requirements, and national regulations.

Cultural Transformation: Organizational mindset shift required to support HIS adoption and digital health practices.

Cybersecurity: Measures taken to protect HIS systems from unauthorized access, breaches, and attacks.

D

Dashboard: A visual tool for monitoring key performance indicators (KPIs) in real time.

Data Governance: Framework ensuring availability, quality, security, and proper use of health information.

Data Integrity: Maintaining completeness, accuracy, and reliability of data throughout its lifecycle.

Decision Rights: Defined authority on who can create, change, or approve data or processes.

Digital Health: Use of information technologies to improve health delivery, patient engagement, and decision support.

Digital Patient Rights: Expanded privacy rights in AI-driven environments where patients control usage, sharing, and revocation of their digital health data.

Dynamic Consent: A flexible consent mechanism allowing patients to modify data permissions over time.

E

EHR (Electronic Health Record): A longitudinal digital record of a patient's medical history, encounters, treatments, and results.

EMR (Electronic Medical Record): A digital chart within a single healthcare organization.

Encryption: Encoding data to prevent unauthorized access during storage or transmission.

F–G

FHIR (Fast Healthcare Interoperability Resources): A modern, API-based standard for exchanging granular healthcare data in real time.

GDPR: European Union regulation governing data privacy, rights, and security.

Governance Committee: A leadership group overseeing HIS policies, data standards, and strategic alignment.

H

Health Information Exchange (HIE): The secure sharing of health data across organizations.

HL7 FHIR (Fast Healthcare Interoperability Resources): is a modern healthcare data standard that enables different systems to share patient information easily and securely using simple, web-based formats.

HL7 v2: Widely adopted legacy messaging standard for exchanging admissions, lab, and clinical data.

HL7 v3: More structured but less widely adopted standard than v2.

Hospital Information System (HIS): The integrated platform supporting clinical, administrative, and financial workflows.

I–L

ICD-10: International coding system for diseases, diagnoses, and external causes.

Intelligent Legal Hold: AI-powered systems that automatically detect litigation triggers and suspend data deletion.

Intelligent Security: Security models that adapt authentication and authorization based on risk signals.

Interoperability: Ability of systems to exchange and interpret shared data consistently.

Learning Health Ecosystem: A HIS paradigm in which data turns into insights, then to action, and then to data, continuously improving care.

LOINC: Standard for coding laboratory and clinical observations.

M–O

NLP (Natural Language Processing): AI technique that transforms unstructured text into structured clinical meaning.

Observation Cycle (CIM): Phase where the team monitors user behavior and system performance.

Organizational Interoperability: Alignment of policies and workflows across departments and institutions to support seamless data exchange.

P

Performance Metrics: Quantitative indicators measuring HIS impact (example: coding accuracy, turnaround times).

Predictive Analytics: AI-driven forecasting of risks, events, or resource needs.

Project Governance: Oversight, ensuring the HIS project aligns with strategy, quality, and compliance.

Q–R

Qualification Cycle (CIM): Phase validating whether implementation outcomes match strategic goals.

Quality Assurance (QA): Activities ensuring HIS modules meet functional, technical, and clinical requirements.

RBAC (Role-Based Access Control): Authorization model granting users access based on roles.

Reliability: Degree to which a system consistently performs as expected.

Resilience: HIS capability to withstand failures or disruptions.

Responsive EMR: EMR that adjusts its interface, alerts, and workflows based on user role, behavior, and context.

S

Scalability: Ability of HIS to support increased users, data, or modules without performance degradation.

Semantic Interoperability: Ensuring that exchanged data has the same meaning across systems.

Smart Hospital (Future Definition): A living and learning node within a wider health ecosystem, connected, agentic, and responsive, a place where data, intelligence, and human purpose interact.

SNOMED CT: Comprehensive clinical terminology supporting detailed clinical expression.

Stakeholder Engagement: Active involvement of clinicians, IT, management, and external partners throughout the HIS lifecycle.

Standardization: Aligning processes, data structures, and workflows across departments.

Structural Interoperability: Ability to parse standardized data formats and store information in correct fields.

System Usability: Degree to which HIS interfaces are intuitive, efficient, and user-centered.

T–V

Telemedicine: Use of digital technologies for remote patient consultations and monitoring.

Usability Testing: Validating system ease of use through real-world testing scenarios

Value Realization: Measurement of how HIS implementation delivers financial, clinical, or operational benefits.

URGENT PLEA!

Thank You For Reading My Book!

I really appreciate all of your feedback and

I love hearing what you have to say.

I need your input to make the next version of this

book and my future books.

Please take two minutes now to leave a helpful review on

My email address: Shahram@dtsage.com, letting me
know what you thought of the book.

Thanks so much

Shahram Gharib

Index